Great Musicians
from our First Nations

Vincent Schilling

Second Story Press

Library and Archives Canada Cataloguing in Publication

Schilling, Vincent, 1967-
Great musicians from our First Nations / by Vincent Schilling.

(The First Nations series for young readers)
Includes bibliographical references.
ISBN 978-1-897187-76-0

1. Indian musicians—Canada—Biography—Juvenile literature. 2. Native
musicians—Canada—Biography—Juvenile
literature. 3. Indian musicians—United States—Biography—
Juvenile literature. I. Title. II. Series: First Nations series
for young readers.

ML3929.S36 2010   780.92'397   C2010-900607-0

Printed on recycled paper in Canada
Co-published in the United States of America

*Second Story Press gratefully acknowledges the support of the Ontario Arts
Council and the Canada Council for the Arts for our publishing program. We
acknowledge the financial support of the Government of Canada through the
Book Publishing Industry Development Program.*

ONTARIO ARTS COUNCIL
CONSEIL DES ARTS DE L'ONTARIO

Canada Council   Conseil des Arts
for the Arts   du Canada

Published by
Second Story Press
20 Maud Street, Suite 401
Toronto, ON
M5V 2M5
www.secondstorypress.ca

I dedicate this book to all of the amazing students, teachers, school officials, and residents of Ronan, Montana, and those I met on the Flathead Indian Reservation.

In 2008, when I visited K. William Harvey Elementary School, Pablo Elementary School, Ronan Middle School, and other places in Ronan, I talked with numerous talented and intelligent people. Because of everyone's kindness, their willingness to face any challenge, and their desire to make positive choices, I was truly inspired and my life was changed forever.

I will never forget the wonderful people that you all are—and will always be. Now go out there and take the world by storm like I know you can. Invest in your heritage and your history—take it with you into the future.

—Vincent Schilling

Vincent Schilling is an award-winning author, photojournalist, speaker, and photographer who lives in Virginia Beach with his wife, Delores.

Vincent has contributed to numerous national and regional publications, including *Indian Country Today*, *Inside Business*, *Tidewater Parent*, and *Tribal College Journal*. He has an incredible passion for photography and loves to travel and visit quirky attractions throughout the country. Together with his wife, he has visited a giant shoe in Pennsylvania, gazed at twenty-foot-tall ducks (not real ones) and a foam replica of Stonehenge in the Shenandoah Valley, and a field of dinosaurs in Connecticut.

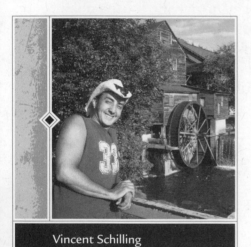

Vincent Schilling

One of his favorite experiences was to meet with Native youth in Ronan, Montana, to talk about his experiences as an author.

CONTENTS

CHAPTER 1

Michael Bucher (CHEROKEE)

CHAPTER 2

Mary Youngblood (SEMINOLE/ALEUT)

CHAPTER 3

Crystal Shawanda (OJIBWA)

CHAPTER 4

Blackfire (NAVAJO)

CHAPTER 5

Leela Gilday (DENÉ)

So many people contributed to the process of creating this book. I would like to thank every one of them, and I will do my best to do so. If I have forgotten anyone, it is nothing other than human error. My gratitude to all is genuine.

First, I would like to thank my best friend and life partner, Delores Schilling. In one way or another, every book I write is dedicated to my wife, who has inspired me and helped me to become what I only could have dreamed to be.

I want to thank everyone at Book Publishing Company. Without the help and input of Kathleen Hanson, Bob Holzapfel, Warren Jefferson, Anna Pope, and others at BPC, gifts to the world such as this book about Native musicians would never materialize. Because of your efforts, many lives can change for the better.

I want to thank my father, Ray Schilling, and Mary Schilling. Thanks for my sense of humor, Dad. I also thank my wife's family, which has taken me under their wing. Thank you Sharon, Mary, and Parker.

I would also like to thank those who have been supportive and helped in the process of this book's creation: Dann Boyko, Kathy Flores, Bill and Doris Anderson, Lynette Allston, the Nottoway Indian Tribe of Virginia, and all my friends at Glazenfyre. Thank you to Ken Polisse and Rob Capriccioso, who have consistently given me great advice, and thanks to Louis O'Reilly, Lori Genes, and Berta Benally, Blackfire's "manager."

I would like to commend Eric Klein of the Can-Do Organization for the work he is doing for Native American reservations in the United States and offer a big thanks to Mary, Gabriel Ayala's mother, who let him keep his guitar.

Most of all, I want to thank the musicians who took time to share intimate details about their lives. This book is certainly about you. Your journeys, as well as mine, have only begun.

PHOTO CREDITS

Page iv: Courtesy of Delores Schilling

Page 1: Courtesy of Debra Bucher

Page 3: Courtesy of Michael Bucher

Pages 8, 9, 27, 29, 31, 60, 64, 74, 85, 88, 92, 94: Courtesy of Vincent Schilling

Pages 11, 17, 20: Courtesy of Catherine Daly

Pages 22, 34: Courtesy of Russ Harrington

Page 36, 40, 46, 48: Courtesy of Blackfire

Pages 50 and 57: Courtesy of Nadya Kwandibens

Page 52: Courtesy of Leela Gilday

Page 77: Courtesy of Tammy Luker

Pages 79 and 81: Courtesy of Pat Evans

Page 83: Courtesy of Melissa Walkup Kennison

Page 96, 98, 99, 103: Courtesy of O'Reilly International

Pages 105, 110, 113: Courtesy of Georgina Anderson

Page 106: Courtesy of Ayala family

KWE KWE. (HELLO HELLO!)

 After deciding with my publishing company to write about the lives of some amazing Native American musicians, little did I know the amazing adventure I would undertake in the course of writing this book.

My process began in early 2008. My first interview was with country musician Shane Yellowbird. His popularity was growing at the time of our conversation and, in the course of a year, has grown a hundredfold.

Later in 2008, I met with Mato Nanji, lead singer of Indigenous. I spent half the day with him and his band members in my hometown of Virginia Beach. We talked about what it was like touring on the road. They said it was tough but fun. I stayed with Mato until the evening and watched as he and his band played some of the best live music I have ever heard for an appreciative crowd.

I was able to hold a conference call with the members of the punk group Blackfire. Their intelligence and insight was more than brilliant. I also spoke and laughed with Leela Gilday, who has an incredible spirit; Jamie Coon, who has truly shown me that Native people have what it takes; and Mary Youngblood, one of the strongest Native women I have ever spoken with. I left each conversation with a better understanding of the lives we live as Native people, and I am a better person for knowing each one of these musicians.

In January 2009, as an author for Book Publishing Company and a journalist for *Indian Country Today*, I traveled to Washington, DC, to cover the 2009 inauguration of President Barack Obama and to Alexandria, Virginia, for the American Indian Society's Inaugural Ball.

. During this historic time, I met with countless leaders, elders, and tribal members from Indian nations all over the country. I interviewed Senator Ben Nighthorse Campbell (you can read about him in my book *Native Men of Courage*) and Chief Lynette Allston of the Nottoway Indian Tribe of Virginia. I also interviewed Mitchell Bush, retired Branch Chief of Tribal Enrollment Services for the Bureau of Indian Affairs; Clayton Old Elk of the Crow Nation; and Buford Rolin, chairman of the Poarch Band of Creek Indians in Alabama; and countless others.

On the morning of the inauguration, I headed out to the parade ground, where the wind chill was minus two degrees, with millions of other people. We walked the streets together and crammed ourselves like sardines into subway cars.

That morning, classical guitarist Gabriel Ayala called to tell me he had recently been in a nearly fatal car crash. I was overwhelmed but sincerely glad that he was recovering well. I promised him that I would mention how his mom almost prevented his career as a classical guitarist by telling him to sell his guitar when he was young. (Sorry, Gabe's mom, a promise is a promise!)

Later that morning, I made my way to the inaugural parade route and stood waiting for long hours in painfully cold weather to see our nation's first president of color travel down Pennsylvania Avenue en route to the White House. The crowd went wild as our new president passed by. I stayed for a few hours longer to photograph the American Indian parade participants and others.

After a long, cold, and exhausting day, I went to see *Native Music Rocks*, a concert featuring Native artists Derek Miller, Martha Redbone, Bill Miller, Micki Free, Levi and the Plateros, and others.

At the concert, I was five feet away from Crystal Shawanda, a country artist who performs with an incredible amount of energy and zest for life. I met with her backstage, and together we spoke with excitement about this book project.

However, the night was not over. I rushed to the American Indian Society's Inaugural Ball and watched Michael Bucher perform with Joanne Shenandoah. I hung out with Michael and his wife, Debra, and learned what an incredible person he is as well as a talented musician and singer.

I had spent three days in the Washington, DC, area and got about four hours of sleep. It was tough, it was crazy, but heck, it was a blast. Besides, I had been a part of history. Who would have thought an author's life could be so exciting?

Perhaps one of my greatest honors came while I was attending a practice session of Four Rivers Drum. The members of this group live in my hometown, and after a series of photographs and interviews, they asked me and my six-year-old nephew, Parker, to sit at the drum and play along. I was grateful and honored to have participated. Later, Michael Cloud-Butler, a member of Four Rivers Drum and now a close friend, told me, "Vincent, you are always welcome to play with us. We consider you a member of this drum." Few greater honors have been bestowed on me in my life.

Lastly, I would like to tell you why I write. I write because I hope to inspire you. I hope to inspire all of my young friends who take the time to read these chapters. When you read these words, attend to them with more than your eyes or ears. If greatness is your desire, then listen with your spirit. Do not ever give up—ever! I write because your life matters to me.

I will make you a promise. If you continue to make positive choices in your life (no matter how big or small they may seem), the universe has no other option than to grant you success.

For example, in 2008 I traveled to Ronan, Montana, and met with students at Ronan Middle School, Pablo Elementary School, and K. William Harvey Elementary School to talk about my first book, *Native Athletes in Action*. I shared the message of "making positive choices" with students. Later, a student told me he had listened to my words and followed my advice. He said a student on the bus was joking around and threw a piece of paper that hit him. He told me he usually responded negatively to such things but decided instead to ignore it. I told him that he had just done an amazing thing and changed the course of his life. It may have seemed minor, but what if he had fought with the other student or responded negatively in some way? Many things could have happened to harm both students. However, because of his seemingly small choice, this student might have averted disaster.

So I say this to you: If you want to achieve greatness, I have the solution. It will solve every problem that you have and will *guarantee* success in your life. Continue to make positive choices, continue to stay on the path that is often not followed by the masses, and stick to your dream even if someone says it is stupid or impossible. Let me tell you, no dream is stupid or impossible.

It is absolutely possible to achieve your dreams. I know you can do it. I know I will see you all at the top of the mountain named Success. I bid you the best in your quest for greatness. When you are there at the top, whether as a great musician, doctor, firefighter, teacher, parent, or as someone who is there when someone needs you, I will be there to shake your hand and give you a well-deserved pat on the back. I will be there to tell you with the utmost sincerity, "I knew you could do it."

Be well my friends. Nia:wen. (Thank you.)

—*Vincent Schilling*

Michael Bucher

VOCALIST AND COMPOSER OF
MUSIC TO PROTECT SACRED SITES

Anyone lucky enough to have a conversation with Michael Bucher is bound to notice this Cherokee musician's joyful attitude and zest for life. He exudes a real sense of friendly welcome, as if he would always be willing to listen to your concerns. Combine this genuine personal warmth with his beautiful music and inspiring call to political action, and a remarkable artist emerges.

Michael Bucher

Born in 1953, Michael can trace his Cherokee ancestors back to the Trail of Tears. Michael and his siblings are only the second generation of his family that was not born in southeast Missouri. Rather than growing up on a reservation, they were raised in a small apartment on the South Side of Chicago in an ethnically diverse neighborhood informally known as "Little Mexico." In fact, Michael's neighborhood contained such a mix of cultures that his first job as a newspaper delivery boy entailed delivering five different newspapers in five different languages—Polish, Spanish, Lithuanian, Russian, and English!

Michael grew up with his Cherokee mother, German father, one brother, and three sisters. He also lived a short distance from his Cherokee grandmother, Emma Wiedefeld, and great-uncle, Frank DuMey. Michael's mother and grandmother believed very strongly in Native values. His grandmother had given birth to all her children at home with the use of midwives, without doctors or painkillers. Her choice raised the eyebrows of many of their neighbors, who were often judgmental of the "Indian family," as they were called, and their values.

When he was three years old, Michael's grandmother decided to move to Wisconsin and begin a small farm. The move was not a sad event, because Michael and his family frequently visited his grandmother on weekends and in the summer. Michael remembers her farm very fondly: "She had chickens, pigs, and a huge garden with herbs and flowers. She even grew her own tobacco." For as long as he can remember, Michael's grandmother and other family members told stories rich with Cherokee teachings about the Creator, animals, and nature. Most of all, they taught him kindness and love, which guided his actions while he was growing up.

In Catholic school in Chicago, Michael spent most of his days wishing he could be with his grandmother on her Wisconsin farm. He recalls, "I would look outside, and I would be daydreaming. School was fine, but I would always rather not be there." His artistic soul did not enjoy learning in the structured environment of school. Instead, he preferred to learn the Indian way, through storytelling.

Michael also loved music, especially the drums. When he was just eight years old, he made his first drum with the help of his grandmother. She taught him that the drum is a sacred vessel—the "heartbeat of the people"—and should not be mistreated or disrespected. To this day, one of his favorite hobbies remains Native-style drum making.

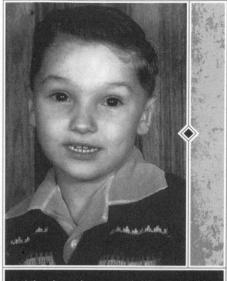

Michael Bucher as a child

His grandmother's drum-making lessons were just part of Michael's musical inspirations. Other musical influences were all around him. His family members were self-taught musicians. His mother and a sister played the piano, and his father played the guitar. His brother, aunts, and uncles played, and he played the accordion. He grew up listening to such country music greats as Johnny Cash and Loretta Lynn. In his teen years, he was drawn to rock and roll and rhythm and blues.

Although his passion for music was strong and his family was always supportive, Michael faced an obstacle that stifled this passion and damaged his self-esteem. As a young Native, he was often subjected to stereotypical Hollywood-style Indian wailing and whooping from his peers. He says, "The only people I could really have good friendships with at the time were the Hispanic people. We were looked at as the lowest people on the block, but that was okay with me. My Hispanic friends and their families were proud people." The fact that Michael and his friends were "in the same boat" strengthened his friendships.

Although Michael did have a few friends to whom he could relate, he felt hurt by the taunting and prejudice he felt from other kids and found it difficult to maintain a sense of self-worth faced with the feeling, as he recalls, of "not being good enough." With his Indian heritage a source of pain for him, he began to feel that being Native American would prevent him from becoming a musician.

But Michael persevered. When he was around thirteen years old, he and some friends formed a band called the Jades, and he played drums with the group. Michael enjoyed the learning process of creating music, but the band was all in fun. At fifteen, Michael joined another group called Last-Minute Rush, which did cover songs of the rock music of the day. This band was a little more serious, and its members were talented enough to get a few local gigs, including some high school dances.

When Michael was sixteen, one night changed his life forever. On this particular evening, he had gone with his cousin to help him with his job cleaning a local fast food restaurant, since the two were planning to go out afterward. However, Michael met another employee at the restaurant, a young woman named Debra. His description of their meeting says it all: "I saw her and I was like, 'Whoa!' It was instant. I know the old saying of love at first sight is totally beaten to death, but, even at that young age, I knew. It hit me like a ton of bricks, like a two by four across the head." Debra and Michael started dating, and after a year, he knew that she was the person with whom he wanted to share the rest of his life. They were married at the young age of seventeen.

Michael decided to set aside music as a career and focus on a different direction in his new life. He tried college for a short time after high school but found it was not a good fit for him; instead he went to work as a full-time metal finisher. However, he did not completely throw away his musical dreams. To keep his artistry alive, he began to learn how to play the guitar on his off time.

When Michael was twenty-one, his beloved grandmother, who had taught him so much about Cherokee traditions and beliefs, passed away. "When she crossed over, I was crushed," remembers Michael. His great-uncle took over as his mentor, helping Michael walk the ways of his ancestors as his grandmother had done. He and Michael got to know each other very well.

In 1973, Michael and Debra had their first son, whom they named Michael Jr. Four years later, their twin sons, Clint and Justin, were born. As his sons grew, Michael continued his livelihood as a metalworker, but after fourteen years of this work, he and Debra decided to move to Wisconsin. They wanted to settle in the area where his grandmother had lived, but land was too expensive there. Instead, they settled in northwestern Wisconsin. Michael was thirty-five years old and starting anew.

In Wisconsin, Michael continued on his path as a caring provider for his family. He worked on and off as a carpenter and held a full-time position in a window factory. Eventually, he left the factory to do carpentry full-time and continued in this line of work for about eleven years. During this time, Michael's relationship with his great-uncle Frank strengthened.

For years, Michael and Frank had been discussing the affairs of Native American people. One particular topic that came up repeatedly was the desecration of Native American sacred sites and burial mounds. Frank told Michael that, at one time, the Cherokee people were not considered full citizens, and as a result, many sacred Cherokee burial sites had been torn apart and robbed by treasure seekers. Equally tragic, nothing could be done about it.

Michael's great-uncle was getting older and he encouraged Michael to take a more serious look at possibly using his music for the Native American cause. Michael remembers his words: "You know, Mike, if you are going to do something, you've got to quit griping and stand up and do something about it. You have this voice, and you have this guitar; do something."

Michael's great-uncle Frank spoke powerful words in his last days. Michael decided to honor them by doing everything in his power to carry the message of protecting sacred sites. Michael's respected elder had given him "the shove," as Michael calls it. At an age when most people would not even consider such a brave move, Michael finally decided to pursue a musical career. He was fifty-two years old at the time.

Over the years, Michael had been writing songs. It was in 2006, at the moment when he decided to pull together ten songs for an album, that Michael's ancestors, as he puts it, "really started speaking and giving me the words and the music and the inspiration." He decided to name the album *Seven*.

Why *Seven*? Michael's grandmother had taught him that when the Cherokee people pray, they give respect to the seven directions. The first four are the cardinal directions: North signifies cold, rebirth, and hibernation; South signifies the origin of warm weather and warm winds; East is where the sun rises, prayers are directed, and doors face; and West signifies the sunset and rain for crops. The remaining three directions are inherent to Cherokee beliefs: everything comes from Father Sky, who brings rain and contains the sun, moon, and stars; everything we have and make comes from Mother Earth, who gives us the soil, trees, and wood; and everything interconnecting the Cherokee people—hearts, souls, and beliefs—comes from the perpetual Fire That Burns Within.

"Cherokee Rose" and other songs were written before Michael decided to put an album together. Writing the rest of the songs for *Seven* was an amazing creative process for him. Armed with the words of his great-uncle and the guidance of his ancestors, he dove headfirst into his music. Michael describes the experience: "At one point, I was writing the song 'Don't Forget about Me' so fast, I literally had to ask my ancestors to slow down, because I couldn't keep up."

After all the songs were written, Michael completed the CD at a recording studio in Chippewa Falls. With one thousand copies from the studio in hand, he set out to distribute them. He admits he really did not know what he was doing. Luckily for him, he got some help. WOJB, a Native radio station at Lac Courte Oreilles Reservation in northwestern Wisconsin where he had volunteered for years, helped him navigate the world of CD promotion. WOJB staff members Camille Lacapa and Nicki Kellar were particularly helpful. With their assistance, and after extensive research, Michael sent his CD to radio stations across the country and into Canada. Within a relatively short time, three songs on his album, "Don't Forget about Me," "Dirty Water," and "Invisible Indian," began receiving airplay in the United States, including Alaska, and in Canada; and Michael began receiving critical acclaim as a musician. "I was so blessed to have the people who were willing to help me," recalls Michael.

About the same time his songs were receiving attention, Michael was invited to WOJB's twenty-fifth anniversary celebration to play along with acclaimed Native American musician Bill Miller. This was his first gig of significance. Others followed, and in 2008 he played with Keith Secola and, once again, Bill Miller, at the Longest Walk in Washington, DC, an event commemorating the original 1978 walk from San Francisco to Washington in support of indigenous sacred sites. Michael remembers an interesting statement from Bill, who had been in the music industry for many years. Bill told him, "I feel sorry for anybody trying to break into music nowadays; it's very difficult. You have to be your own person and not rely on anyone else to do it for you. You've really got to get out there and do it yourself."

Michael heeded Bill's advice. Within one year of becoming a musician and "getting out there," he received two

Nammy nominations at the 2007 Ninth Annual Native American Music Awards for Best Debut Artist and Best Folk Recording for "Don't Forget about Me." Here he was, in his midfifties, and Michael was just beginning to live his dream.

Although he was gaining recognition as a musician, Michael did not forget the words of his great-uncle, who had passed on, imploring him "to do something" to bring awareness to Native American sacred sites and burial grounds. Michael concentrated specifically on Bear Butte Mountain, a site sacred to the Lakota, Dakota, and Nakota people in South Dakota. He began working on a music video for his song "Dirty Water" to address the importance of preserving the lands of Bear Butte, which are threatened by the continued development of the nearby Sturgis Motorcycle Rally. The video received national recognition and a Nammy nomination in 2008 at the Tenth Annual Native American Music Awards for Best Short Form Video.

Michael Bucher performs with Joanne Shenandoah on Inauguration Day

Michael's next politically driven video dealing with the protection of Native sacred sites was "Don't Forget about Me," taped in 2008 at the Black Hills Wild Horse Sanctuary near Hot Springs, South Dakota. A popular film production location, the sanctuary is a sprawling, nonprofit enterprise in operation since 1988. The song itself, "Don't Forget about Me," earned a nomination and went on to win the award for Best Political Song at the 2008 First Annual Native-E Music Awards.

Michael Bucher on Inauguration Day

Success has not necessarily stopped Michael's battles with his self-esteem as a musician. He explains, "Being nominated for the Nammys is the fun part, but then that same haunt comes back. 'I'm not as good as these guys, those artists are incredible, these men and women have been doing this their whole life, and who am I?' Those are the hardest things to squash." But Michael turns his doubts into fun and creativity by continuing to work. In 2008, he put together an album with Joanne Shenandoah titled *Bitter Tears, Sacred Ground*, which was released at the American Indian Inaugural Ball on January 20, 2009. He is also putting together a new album, named *Believe*, which will continue his focus on sacred sites of the Native American people. According to Michael, "I've got a lot more to say and a lot more people to help, hopefully."

Michael is hoping that *Believe* will have the kind of effect that *Seven* had. For example, the song "You Are Not Alone" from the album has touched many lives. Michael says, "I cannot tell you how many emails I get about that song.

People thank me for those words. People say they have played that song every day and have gotten through their hard times. There is a Native woman from Canada who wakes up and plays my song every day, which helps her attitude at work. Those things give me goose bumps. When I read these words, I thank the Creator."

With everything in perspective, Michael gives advice to those interested in his journey: "My life has not been a bowl of cherries. Like many Native people, I've struggled with the demons, be it alcohol, depression, or whatever." He advises young people to stay true to their purpose, saying, "Hopefully you will find that battle that you have to fight, and if you do find it, fight it well, and stay true to your intentions."

As a musician pursuing his calling later than most, Michael feels blessed. With passion and determination, and inspired by the teachings of his elders, he has brought about awareness of the sacred sites and burial grounds of Native Americans. He also has given the world some amazing music. Despite his late start, Michael Bucher is certain to delight and inspire his fans for many more years to come while spreading the important message of protecting the sacred sites of indigenous people. A sampling of the lyrics of "You Are Not Alone" speaks to the inspiration that he imparts to his people: "Just stand by me and I'll stand by you / together we can do this / we're not alone."

Contact Michael Bucher
P.O. Box 181
Birchwood, WI 54817
Website: www.michaelbucher.com
Email: seven@indianheadtel.net

Mary Youngblood

NATIVE AMERICAN FLUTIST

The age-old story of a struggling artist whose life is full of difficulties certainly rings true for Mary Youngblood. Mary has had her share of obstacles, yet she was both determined and able to conquer them and go on to become a two-time Grammy-winning musician.

Mary was born in Seattle, Washington, in 1958. She was adopted when she was seven months old by non-Indian parents. Her father, Bob Edwards, was a high school English teacher and her mother, Leah, was a homemaker.

Young Mary and her family lived in Kirkland, a small town in Washington. Although Bob and Leah were loving parents, their interests were firmly rooted in the classical arts rather than in Native American culture. The family did not watch much television, so Mary learned to find other enjoyable things to do, such as exploring the open countryside and picking berries off the bushes.

Mary Youngblood

The activities Mary found to keep herself busy did not prevent her from noticing early in her life that she was different. She began to feel a sense of exclusion in her predominantly white neighborhood and was often teased because she did not look like her parents or her sisters. She knew she was Native American—although she did not know what tribe either of her birth parents was from—and her adoptive parents tried to help her connect to her heritage. Together they read books about Native Americans and visited museums to expose her to her culture. These efforts, however, could not erase the fact that, as Mary describes it, "I stood out like a sore thumb in that community—it was really tough being brown in a white world."

Mary suffered terribly in elementary school. During the middle of fourth grade, she and her family moved so her father could pursue his doctorate degree. Her new schoolmates treated her badly, sometimes to the point of beating her up. When they chased her home, she would hide in the bushes. Ridiculed in the classroom and terrified of the walk to and from school, Mary had to go to counseling. Desperate to bring happiness into her life, she turned to the arts for a source of comfort.

The arts provided a way for Mary to be able to express herself, to be able to go inward and be creative. She had already displayed a natural ability on the piano when she was only six years old. But in the fourth grade, in the midst of all her unhappiness and suffering, she chose the instrument that would be her destiny. Or rather, it chose her. For in reality, she wasn't excited to learn to play the classical flute. But because the school year was already half over, the only instrument left in band was the flute, an instrument that, as Mary says, "you can't even look at when you play."

Undeterred, she decided to make the best of her situation. With her parents' encouragement, she embraced the flute and began to improve with practice. Her father signed her up for private flute lessons at the university where he worked, and Mary began to excel as a musician.

As she continued to get better with the flute, she found her life also improving. By the time she reached high school, things were not as difficult for her as they had been, although they were not altogether easy. The family had moved again, to Fair Oaks, California, where Mary attended a predominantly white high school. To ward off her feelings of seclusion and loneliness—including that feeling of being out of place that is so difficult for a teenager—she became more deeply involved with the arts, pouring her emotions into them.

The arts not only were healing for her, they also saved her from making self-destructive choices. During this time, in the 1970s, drug use among her peers was very common. But instead of following this destructive path as some of her friends did, Mary chose to make positive and constructive choices, keeping alive her big dream to succeed and be someone special. She deepened her involvement with art, branching out into sculpture and painting, particularly landscape oil painting, which she still enjoys today.

Mary also broadened her embrace of music. By now, she played the piano, violin, classical flute, and guitar. She joined a band called the American Truckin' Company, directed by Tony Logan, a youth minister. In the band, Mary played the classical flute and the guitar and sang back-up vocals. The band traveled around the community performing at events such as high school dances and weddings. These years were not only exciting and fun for Mary, but they were also important for her personal growth. At one point, she even played music with the then unknown actor LeVar Burton at the Holiday House Nightclub in Grass Valley, California. Mr. Burton had just finished production of *Roots*, the famous TV miniseries.

During her senior year, Mary began dating. After high school graduation, she started working, and soon afterward, young and unprepared as she was, she got married. Before long she found herself with two children, Benjamin and Elizabeth, and a husband who was heavily involved with drugs and alcohol. One day, Mary's husband left and never came back. She had no choice but to go on welfare.

Mary remembers those years when her children were young as being tough times. With no car, she found that picking up her food stamps was difficult enough. Carrying groceries with the kids and a stroller in tow was really challenging. Fortunately, Mary had an elderly neighbor, Mrs. Smith, with whom she developed a friendship. A former nurse, Mrs. Smith was alone, and although she no longer could drive, she still had her car. With Mary driving, they would go get food stamps together, and Mrs. Smith would sit with the kids while Mary went inside to pick them up at a place that Mary describes as "horrible." At a time when Mary was a scared new mom, Mrs. Smith, in Mary's own words, "saved my spirit."

During these hard times, Mary held fast to her dreams of becoming someone special. She still had her musical instrument, a Gemeinhardt silver flute. Although she pawned it repeatedly during those years, she always retrieved it before the end of her six-month deadline of being able to reclaim it. She also kept a journal and wrote both songs and short stories to offset her sadness. It was important for Mary to nurture the creative process and, in hindsight, those hard times turned out to be precious years, beneficial for her creative growth.

Making the best of her situation, Mary made her small home cheerful and developed friendships with her neighbors. In time, Mary remarried and had two more children, Joseph and Christopher. Her new husband was a counselor, and Mary became a licensed daycare provider. Life was beginning to improve for her and her family. She even became a Cub Scout leader.

It was at this time in her life that fate intervened to connect Mary—a struggling mother in her thirties—with her heritage. Across the street from her home was a New Age store that sold such items as rocks, stones, and crystals. One day when she was in the store, the owner approached her and asked if she was a Native American and if she had ever played a Native American flute. She had not, but she picked it up and started to play.

To her surprise, playing this flute came very easily to her. People in the store stopped to listen, and when she was finished, they applauded. What a weird experience this was for Mary—she had never touched a Native American flute, she had never heard Native American music, and yet, as Mary puts it, "I had just made music!"

The storeowner let her put the flute on a payment plan. Mary worked at an art gallery, and she began to play there. Soon, word of her talent spread throughout her community. Eventually, some Native American friends told Mary that they were putting together an event at a local junior college called Indigenous Peoples' Day, in lieu of a Columbus Day celebration, and invited her to play. Mary was not sure how to respond to the invitation. Although it was clear that people liked what they were hearing when she played, she insisted that she was only making things up as she went along. But when her friends told her that her performance at Indigenous Peoples' Day would pay $250 for twenty minutes, she was convinced. After only thirty-eight days of playing the Native American flute, she was now a paid professional!

Mary's good luck continued as her connection to her Native roots strengthened. She had been working closely with the Adoptees' Liberty Movement Association, which provides assistance in finding adopted children's birthparents. In 1986, after years of research and investigative work, she received a letter with the addresses and phone numbers of her biological family members, including her birth mother. Mary called, and within five minutes, she was talking to her mother.

Mary describes that emotional experience: "It was very surreal. I barely even remember the conversation. I was in shock. I remember her apologizing profusely. She had such a hard time. I was just trying to tell her I was glad I had found her and it was okay. I was just shaking like a leaf. We talked for about an hour, and she put me on the phone with my half-sister, Hannah. It was really wild."

Over time Mary's relationship with her newfound natural family strengthened. They exchanged pictures and birthday cards, and eventually, with help from her adoptive parents, Mary traveled by train with her five-year-old son, Benjamin, to meet them. The trip from Sacramento to Seattle was five hundred miles and took twenty hours. This was an exciting visit for Mary; she discovered that she was one of twelve children and had many other relatives. She met Hannah, who in time became one of her best friends, and a half-brother, and was delighted to discover their shared physical traits. "We had the same toes!" said Mary.

Mary now had a family she hadn't even known about, and the long distance separating them did not keep them from growing closer. She learned that her father was Seminole and her mother Aleut. Her mother had struggled with alcoholism for many years but was able to spend the last four years of her life sober. This was a story with a beautiful ending for Mary, and she recalls her relationship with her mother fondly. Even though she remembers the pain of being separated from her blood family and being disconnected from her culture for well over twenty years, Mary finds she has no regrets.

During this period of family discovery, music continued to be an important element in her life. She discovered a CD composed of flute music titled *Beyond Words*. The music inspired her to practice more diligently. Native people began to ask her to perform at various functions. Growing in both ambition and confidence, she traveled to other states, performing at Native American powwows and elders' day events.

With her musical reputation growing, Mary was invited to perform on a powwow cruise to Ensenada in Baja California,

Mary Youngblood

Mexico. Also booked on the cruise was a singer named Joanne Shenandoah. Mary thought her voice was beautiful and contacted the cruise director to ask about the possibility of meeting her and seeing if their music would work together. When they were introduced to each other on the cruise, they hit if off immediately. In fact, Joanne asked Mary if she would be interested in working on a project in northern California with her, to which Mary enthusiastically replied yes.

At the same time that Mary was becoming friends with Joanne, she began to run into criticism related to her music—not for the quality of her playing but for the instrument she played: the flute. She was told by Native people, even those in her own community, that it was not "traditional" for women to play the flute—that only men play the flute. Mary rejected this criticism, explaining that the tradition was from the Lakota, and she was neither a Southwest nor a Plains Indian. Having grown up in California, she knew that some California Indians played a similar instrument, a small whistlelike tube with three or four holes. Mary stood up for her right to be the first woman to play the Native American flute: "I caught a lot of flack for that. Creator gave me this gift, and I will use that gift to honor Creator and my people. And that is traditional."

Then something wonderful happened. She was at work in the art gallery when a man named Lew Price, an author of multiple books about the design and dynamics of Native American flutes, approached her with an interesting offer. He told her he had heard about her and wanted to make flutes specially designed for her. Part Cherokee and a true scientist, Lew began making flutes that were, in Mary's words, "absolutely and totally and perfectly in pitch."

Mary's playing took a leap forward. She started creating music that did not adhere to the traditional norms generally heard in Native flute compositions. Feeling ready to expand her musical horizons, Mary submitted demo tapes to six record companies. She got a response from five of them. As advised by her friend Joanne Shenandoah, she signed with Joanne's label, Silver Wave Records. The president of Silver Wave had been hesitant to sign her at first because of his concern over the glut of flutists in the market, but he lost his hesitation after hearing her play.

It wasn't long after Mary began working with Silver Wave that she created her first solo flute album, *The Offering*. It was recorded in Moaning Cavern in Calaveras County, the largest one-room cavern in California. Silver Wave set up its recording equipment in the cavern, sight unseen, and took a chance on the incredible acoustics. The sound of water plunking in the background turned out to be a wonderful contribution to the music.

Mary was elated to have completed an album, but she was eager to create more music that was even less mainstream and more outside of the preconceived notions about flute composing and playing. She wanted to implement more vocals and piano, alto flute, and classical flute into the mix and had to fight with her record label for these changes. Her next two albums, *Heart of the World* and *Beneath the Raven Moon*, reflected the evolution of her music.

To Mary's incredible excitement, Silver Wave Records submitted *Beneath the Raven Moon* to the National Academy of Recording Arts and Sciences for a Grammy nomination. The album was accepted as a possible nominee and, after a short and nervous wait with her record company, family, and friends, she learned that *Beneath the Raven Moon* made the first cut of fifteen finalists for Best Native American Music Album. Now it was another waiting game for two more months.

In the meantime, Mary had the fun and privilege of being able to vote for her musical peers and favorite artists, musicians like James Taylor. She invited her parents to give their advice about the best conductor of classical music. The initial ballot was required to be submitted online, but the final ballot had to be on paper. Mary signed it, put her assigned number in the box, and sent it off "with prayers and my eagle feather."

Two months later, she was awakened by a phone call from her record producer. Much to her amazement, *Beneath the Raven Moon* was one of five finalists for a Grammy in its category. Screaming and dancing, she woke up her kids and called her parents and anyone else she could think of: "I did it! I am a nominee!"

In spite of receiving this acknowledgement of her talent, Mary was still having financial difficulties. In order to attend the Grammy Awards ceremony, she had to sell a flute. But any difficulties were quickly forgotten when Mary took part in the ceremony—walking down the red carpet, receiving a beautiful Tiffany box containing the nominee pendant, and meeting conductors and classical musicians.

During the pretelevised portion of the ceremony, Mary sat with her group and waited while the nominees of the different musical categories were announced. At last the Native

Accepting the Emmy for the producers of The Spirit of Sacajawea, a documentary for which Mary composed the music.

American category came up. She watched with anticipation as her album was flashed on the gigantic screen, visible to the entire audience. The envelope was passed and opened. Mary, overwhelmed, heard the announcement: "And the winner is, Mary Youngblood for *Beneath the Raven Moon!*"

The audience stood up and cheered. In a state of disbelief, Mary walked up to the stage and accepted her award. Backstage, she shook as the media asked her how it felt to be the first Native American woman to win a Grammy. She was photographed and then was able to call her parents, kids, and the president of her record label before being whisked back to her seat. In tears, she watched the best concert she had ever seen in her life, including Simon and Garfunkel singing "The Sound of Silence." After the ceremony, she attended an over-the-top party in a giant tent decorated with six-foot ice sculptures.

On the flight home from the ceremony, Mary's friend told one of the flight attendants about the Grammy win. Mary pulled out her flute and played for the passengers over the intercom, receiving a standing ovation. When she got off the plane in her hometown of Sacramento, journalists and TV reporters were there to greet her. She was entering new territory as a musician.

On a creative roll, Mary put out another album, *Feed the Fire*, which also received a Grammy nomination. When her fifth and latest album, *Dance with the Wind*, was nominated, Mary, now an established and honored musician, was able to attend the Grammy Awards ceremony under much more comfortable circumstances than her first time around. She and her family rented a limousine and stayed in a beautiful hotel, and it was worth it—*Dance with the Wind* earned Mary her second Grammy, and she once again felt honored and elated.

For Mary the music business has been a wild ride, from the early days of her childhood when she first began to dream big dreams, to having the privilege of working with well-known and respected musicians, to the ultimate honor of twice receiving the most prestigious music award from her fellow musicians.

She encourages everyone to dream big and have huge fantasies. She recalls how, as a youth, she was riveted to all kinds of events that bestow the top honors and highest awards to the contenders, no matter the type of competition—Wimbledon, the Olympics, the Oscars, the Grammys, even the Miss America Pageant. Anytime anyone won the award or trophy as the best at something, she closed her eyes and imagined herself in that role, bending down to have the medal placed around her neck, walking up the stairs to receive her Oscar, having the crown placed on her head.

When the little adopted girl with the big dreams stood onstage not once but twice to accept her Grammy Award, she became a living testament that even the biggest dreams can come true. Today Mary Youngblood continues to make beautiful music.

Contact Mary Youngblood

Website: www.maryyoungblood.com or www.maryyoungblood.net
To contact Mary, sign up on the website.

Crystal Shawanda

COUNTRY MUSIC SINGER

At an age when most people are not even thinking about what career path to choose, Crystal Shawanda knew what she wanted to do. She began composing poetry when words first started making sense to her and wrote her first song at the age of nine. From that point forward, Crystal dedicated her life to pursuing her musical interests. Today, Crystal is an internationally acclaimed country music artist.

Crystal Shawanda

A member of the Ojibwa group, Crystal was born in Ontario, Canada, and raised on the Wikwemikong Reserve, which lies on the eastern side of Manitoulin Island in Lake Huron. She feels that being a Native growing up on the reserve made her automatically "country." On the reserve, life seemed hopeless for many, and she saw many of her cousins and family friends suffer from addictions, alcoholism, and suicide. But they did have music, which Native people have traditionally used as a form of prayer and a way of giving thanks. Crystal describes music as "our everything," and for her it was her salvation. With it, she was able to find the freedom she sought.

Her songwriting ability made itself apparent early. When she was young, Crystal would watch and listen to her mother sing along to Loretta Lynn. Crystal would also sing songs, but they were songs she had made up. One day in particular, she was going about her business in the house when her mother noticed her singing. She asked Crystal where she had heard the song before. Crystal replied that she honestly didn't know, that it had "just popped into my head and I just started to sing." Her mom encouraged her to write it down, telling Crystal that if neither of them had ever heard it before, then Crystal had just written a song. Crystal did write it down, little realizing that the conversation with her mother may have sparked her career as a country singer.

Although Crystal was a happy child, life on the reservation was tough. She enjoyed the strong sense of unity felt among her family and friends, but Wikwemikong was a small, semi-isolated community, and she longed to explore the world outside Manitoulin Island. When her father's north-south route as a truck driver took him from Michigan straight through to Nashville, Tennessee, she saw an opportunity to travel. She asked her father if she could come along for the ride. He was supportive of Crystal's dreams, so he loaded the family into the truck and away they went.

Crystal was amazed at the sights and sounds of Nashville. Known as Music City USA because of its prominent place in the music industry, particularly country music, the city also has a lively music club scene. As the family walked along Broadway, the downtown street dotted with honky-tonks catering to country music fans, Crystal and her family came upon one of the most famous of these establishments, Tootsies Orchid Lounge.

At the time, Crystal was all of eleven years old, but she can recall the event clearly: "I remember standing outside of

WHAT IS A HONKY-TONK?

Many country music enthusiasts know Tootsies Orchid Lounge as the epitome of a honky-tonk. In fact, the *Guinness Book of World Records* lists Tootsies as "The World's Most Famous Honky-Tonk." The dictionary defines the term as "an inexpensive, noisy night-club." However, the actual origin of the term is unknown. A 1900 article in the *New York Sun* employed the term honky-tonk when describing a group of cowboys responding to the sight and sound of a flock of honking geese instead of to the music show they came to see. Whatever the origin of its name, a good honky-tonk should provide its customers with some hard-hitting country music.

Tootsies' front window. I remember how much I wanted to sing." Crystal and her family walked into Tootsies and listened to the band that was playing. She remembers thinking, "If I get up and sing and it's not good enough, then I won't have anything to dream about anymore and nothing to look forward to." She was too afraid to ask if she could sing, and she "just chickened out." She spent the entire ride home with her family regretting not singing at Tootsies.

Crystal was not about to give up. She appealed to her father to travel with him to Tennessee again, and they went there together on several occasions. When she was thirteen, they once again made their way to Tootsies, and this time she was determined not to miss her opportunity. Her father had told her that if she wanted to sing, she would have to go up to the band and ask for herself. She did just that. According to Crystal, "I walked up to the singer and I asked, 'Hey, can I get up to sing?' I got up and I did one song." The band's drummer enjoyed her singing and appealed to the band's singer to let Crystal sing again. Crystal says, "I sang another song, and I got a standing ovation. I was hooked for life. I knew right then and there that I would be back." As if that weren't amazing enough, it turns out that the drummer playing that night was Richard "Sticks" Stickley, a former drummer for Loretta Lynn.

From that point forward, Crystal made every effort to get back to Nashville as often as possible. During one of her trips there with her father, she recorded and released her first single on an independent, compilation CD. The experience of recording but failing to generate any interest made her realize there was a lot more to the music business than she had imagined. She decided she needed to study music at a professional level.

There was no music program on the Wikwemikong Reserve, but Crystal did not treat her situation as an obstacle. Instead she addressed it as a challenge and went to work. She researched and found a school with a recording studio that was a few hours away from her home. She also found grants that would support her studies at the school and would even provide money so she could rent a room. She presented the concept to her parents as if it were a business plan. At first, they were hesitant to allow their thirteen-year-old daughter to move away from home. However, they saw how serious Crystal was about pursuing music, and they eventually agreed to allow her to attend the school.

Some young people have an unhappy home life and are only too glad to leave their families. For Crystal, however, it was the exact opposite. She recalls, "I loved my family and I loved my home and my community. It was the ultimate sacrifice, but I knew in my heart, even at a young age, it was for the best." Crystal wanted to be prepared for her future and looked at school as a stepping-stone. So off she went. "Besides," she says, "it was a few hours closer to Nashville!"

For three years, Crystal attended Korah Collegiate and Vocational School in Sault Ste. Marie, Ontario, for their music program. She was thrilled to learn about different aspects of music, including music theory and studio recording. She also improved her guitar skills in guitar classes. However, after finishing her music curriculum, Crystal dropped out of high school at the age of sixteen and moved to Nashville to pursue her musical career.

This was a decision that Crystal would regret. She remembers the struggle, saying, "I did the unthinkable. It was probably the biggest mistake of my life, because you cannot get a good job when you do not have an education. Life is not a fairy tale. Being out in the world is definitely hard when you are working for minimum wage. That in itself can frustrate you to the point of just giving up."

She did the best she could, working multiple part-time jobs while trying to get singing gigs. But making ends meet was very difficult, and she was often unable to make enough money at her jobs. When she could not get a gig, she sang for tips, which was not a dependable source of income. For a period of five years, Crystal was barely able to make enough money to survive. To make matters worse, she was often homesick and moved back and forth from Ontario to Tennessee multiple times.

In 2002, Crystal finally decided that she would move permanently to Nashville. She said to herself, "You know what? I am moving to Nashville for good because this is who I am. This is what I love to do. If, in fifteen years, I'm still singing for tips on Broadway in downtown Nashville, then it's been a good life."

Once Crystal made the move permanent, things seemed to go her way. For one thing, she got a permanent gig at Tootsies. Not that this automatically made her a star, but it gave her an opportunity, and no matter how difficult things were for Crystal, she refused to admit defeat. She not only had a regular slot singing at Tootsies, but she also spent all her free time there. Whenever there was an additional opening to perform, she was there, waiting to fill in. Crystal explains, "I used to take a nap in the office upstairs. I did not want to leave in case an opening spot came along. Things would happen. People quit, people canceled, or people's cars would break down. For me, it was good old-fashioned hard work."

The other thing that gave her a boost was meeting DeWayne Strobel. DeWayne was playing in a band at Tootsies and approached Crystal, saying, "You are a star. I would be honored to play guitar behind you." Crystal remembers replying, "Well, I don't know about the guitar-playing part, but I'll give you a call." This was the beginning of their relationship, and eventually DeWayne did become Crystal's guitarist. Crystal remembers how they worked together and relied on tips to pay their rent and to make ends meet: "It seems like just yesterday we were being evicted and looking at the tip jug with $20 in it, wondering how we were going to get a new apartment." Within six months, Crystal and DeWayne had fallen in love and were married. Although things were tough for them financially, Crystal was happy with her new husband and still excited to pursue her musical career.

Crystal's perseverance in the face of difficulties made failure almost impossible. By picking up the slots of artists unable to make their performances at Tootsies and by continuously putting herself out in the public's eye, she began to be noticed. She and DeWayne started to get attention on Music Row, Nashville's music-business community. She explains, "We built up a following. We had writers, publishers, and producers coming to see our show. Not everybody would approach us, but there was a buzz about us."

Crystal Shawanda

One memorable night, a music producer by the name of Scott Hendricks walked into Tootsies. Crystal was singing "Your Cheatin' Heart," by Hank Williams. Mr. Hendricks, who has produced such artists as Faith Hill, Brooks and Dunne, Trace Adkins, and Alabama, stood right in front of the stage, watched, and listened. When she finished singing, he held out his hand and introduced himself, explaining that he had been hearing a lot of buzz about her and that the buzz was right. Crystal remembers this introduction, which changed her life, very clearly, because Mr. Hendricks said, "I think I can get you a record deal." But Crystal had heard this line before, so she proceeded with care. She asked Mr. Hendricks to stick around until after the show so they could talk. She wanted to hear what his goals were for her music and what direction he envisioned taking it. He agreed, and when they sat down together, she told him her goals and visions.

Although Crystal was meeting with a top producer in the music industry, someone whom almost any musician would love to meet, she was cautious. She knew a lot of people thought she was crazy—"That's Scott Hendricks, sign with him!"—but she had waited almost her whole life for this opportunity, and she wanted to make sure he was the right producer for her. She says, "You have to look before you jump. You could be working with the best people in the world, but the bottom line is that everyone wants to get the best deal they can get, no matter how good a person they are."

So, in spite of her eagerness to sign with Scott Hendricks, Crystal practiced patience. Together they decided to hone her skill to create a finely polished product. They went into the studio and recorded several songs until they found the perfect three songs for her. Then they pitched them to RCA Records. The record company people thought she was great but wanted to hear her perform live before they talked business.

Motivated by RCA's interest, Crystal held a showcase before a live audience to demonstrate her talent. The head of RCA Records (now Sony/BMG) in Nashville, Joe Galante, came to the showcase. Crystal gave the audience a show to remember. Mr. Galante was impressed and asked for another showcase. He not only paid for it but also invited his entire staff to watch Crystal perform. After witnessing another impressive performance, he approached the stage and said to Crystal, "Welcome to the family."

Finally, after all those years of hard work, Crystal had a record deal. But record deals—at least good ones—do not happen instantaneously. Crystal knew that more patience was needed before the deal would be complete. She explains, "If you sign on the dotted line right on the spot, you are a fool." After Mr. Galante offered her the record deal, it took another two months before the contract was actually signed. First it went to her lawyer, who looked it over with Crystal. Together they crossed off what we they did not like and then sent it back. "And," Crystal says, "that is when the fun begins, because it goes back and forth between lawyers." It took all concerned another two months to come up with something that everyone agreed upon. During this time, Crystal practiced patience and caution, being very careful to make the right decisions, holding fast to her belief that "everything good takes time. When I hear about people who signed a record contract right on the spot, I think either they lied or they got a really bad deal."

After her record deal with RCA Records was finally secured, Crystal released her

Crystal Shawanda performs for an excited crowd in Washington, DC, for "Native Music Rocks" on the night of the 2009 Presidential Inauguration

debut single, "You Can Let Go," in Canada, in January 2008. It became the fastest-climbing single on the Canadian Country Singles Chart since Carolyn Dawn Johnson's "Georgia" in 2000, reaching top-ten status in just five weeks. A few months later, the single was released in the United States to rave reviews. In the meantime, Crystal got to work producing her first album. As a preview to its release, in February 2008, Country Music Television Canada aired a six-part series called *Crystal: Living the Dream*, which documented Crystal's rise to fame.

Dawn of a New Day, Crystal's first album, was released on August 19, 2008. It entered the Canadian Country Albums chart at number two and the Billboard Country Albums chart at number sixteen, making Crystal the highest-charting full-blooded Native American country artist in the Nielsen Sound-Scan era. (SoundScan is an information system, begun in March 1991, that tracks music and video sales in the United States and Canada.)

For a musician, awards and nominations often follow recognition of talent through sales, and Crystal was no exception. The 2008 Aboriginal Peoples Choice Music Awards presented her with three awards out of five nominations: Best New Artist, Best Country CD for *Dawn of a New Day*, and Single of the Year for "You Can Let Go." Perhaps even more exciting for Crystal were her five wins out of five nominations at the 2008 Canadian Aboriginal Music Awards. She took home Best Female Artist, Best Album of the Year, Best Country Album, Best Music Video, and Best Song Single.

Winning eight prestigious music awards is a long way from singing for a few dollars in a tip jar at Tootsies Orchid Lounge. But not surprisingly, Crystal still finds her way back, on occasion, to perform at her old stomping ground. And, in this case, the term stomping ground can be applied literally, because when Crystal sings, she stomps her feet to the music. In fact, she once stomped her foot so hard that her heel became stuck in Tootsies' stage floor. When she pulled up her foot to release her shoe, the heel broke off and remained stuck.

Stomping is Crystal's way of getting into the music. She attributes her stomping to two different sources: her husband, DeWayne, and her Native upbringing. The passionate way DeWayne plays his guitar inspires her not to care about how she looks while performing. She's come to believe that "you should get lost in what you love." Her second reason harks back to when she was a little girl and a powwow dancer in the style known as Fancy Shawl. Every time she gets on stage, it takes her back to dancing at powwows, when dancing to the beat and stomping on the ground made her close to Mother Earth. She says twirling around and stomping on the stage is the same thing for her now: "I feel like I am right where I am supposed to be. It is the time when I feel closest to God the Creator."

Crystal Shawanda truly sings from her heart. She believes, "You should get lost in what you love."

Two songs on her album, *Dawn of a New Day*, have deep meaning for Crystal. She says the first time songwriters pitched "You Can Let Go" to her, she was transported in "a million different directions." It took her home to her youth and to moving away when she was only thirteen. Looking back now, she realizes she forced herself and her parents to let go of each other a lot sooner than they were ready. Although she admits that if she had the chance to do it all over again she would do it the same way, she does feel some regrets. She knows it was her choice, but she also knows she grew up too fast.

"You Can Let Go" also reminded her of her grandfather, who had many health problems toward the end of his life.

DAWN OF A NEW DAY

Crystal is grateful for the words of her parents. The lyrics of "Dawn of a New Day" seem to pay tribute to her father, whose favorite saying was "Keep on rolling and hope for the best."

> The wind is at my back
> That horizon's calling me
> Gotta keep on rollin'
> Keep on going
> Keep on movin'
> Like a runaway train
> My heart's wide open
> And I ain't slowing down
> Till the sun hits my face
> In the dawn of a new day

Crystal says, "I was almost afraid to sing this song because I did not want to speak it into existence, but in the end my grandfather passed away." Letting go of him was one of the great heartaches of Crystal's life, because he had been such a big part of her moving to Nashville. Ever since she can remember, her grandfather repeatedly said that someday she would live in Nashville and sing at the Grand Ole Opry. Crystal says her grandfather never questioned how she was going to do it. Instead, she says, "there simply was no doubt in his mind."

The single "Dawn of a New Day," from the identically titled album, is also meaningful to Crystal. Her last name, Shawanda, actually translates to this phrase. She views the song as being about her journey to Nashville, because it is a song about hope. The song's lyrics, "You just got to keep on rolling, till the sun hits your face," are about hanging in there, about persevering, as Crystal says, "through the bad stuff to get to those good days." She reminds herself of one of her truck-driving dad's sayings: "The whole world could be falling apart, and he would just be standing there with a little smile on his face and saying, 'You've got to keep on rolling and hope for the best.'" Her mother expresses it differently but with the same positive attitude, saying, "Just trust your path." Crystal considers herself lucky to have had her parents' positive attitudes handed down to her.

On the path to superstardom, Crystal earned the credential to dish out advice and talk about what it takes to succeed in life. She feels that everyone deserves to be a winner no matter what circumstances they come from or what has happened in their lives. She describes herself as having "fallen into the wrong lifestyle" and making many mistakes: "I have made a lot of wrong turns and wrong choices. It is human nature, and I'll probably make more in the future. But I never stop trying to do what's right and never stop trying to be the best that I can be." She advises people to forget about the mistakes they made in the past, to ignore what other people think, and to find out what they love and then pursue that. She emphasizes being positive, open-minded, and openhearted, saying, "You get so much further in your life if you do that."

Being Native American exposed Crystal to more than her share of tragedy. As far back as she can remember, she saw family and friends succumb to the disease of alcoholism. She lived with a lot of death around her at a young age—suicides and alcohol-related deaths like car accidents and drownings—and understood it "a lot better than I should have." So she knows from personal experience what it is like to lose hope and to feel like the rest of the world does not know that you even exist.

She was not immune to this hopelessness. During one of her trips to Nashville, a professional music figure told her that within the music industry "they didn't see Native Americans and country music ever happening." Crystal didn't get offended; she just took it as this one person's honest opinion. But in truth, she carried that statement around "in the back of my heart and in the back of my head." After a couple of years of running from it, the message caught up with her and she temporarily lost hope. She gave up on herself and self-doubt sunk in. One day, "by the grace of God," she changed her way of thinking. She realized there was no reason to give up her dream and her happiness because of one person's opinion. She decided that if she did not succeed, maybe she still could be "a small break within a wall in encouraging young people." That, she says, would make it all worth it: "The way I look at it is that I owe it to myself. And I owe it to those who didn't have the choices that we have today."

Crystal Shawanda

Crystal hopes that young people see all the choices and opportunities they have today that their Native ancestors did not have. She recognizes this cultural shift when she thinks about an uncle of hers who was an amazing singer. Back in his day, he could not even begin to dream about pursuing a musical career and becoming a famous singer. Crystal explains that "a lasting result of the residential-school era was a defeated mentality and a lingering lack of self-esteem." For her uncle, pursuing a musical career and becoming a famous singer was "a dream of improbability" when he was growing up.

The proof now exists that a Native American and Aboriginal Canadian woman can indeed make it in country music. The proof lies in Crystal Shawanda, who has risen up against incredible odds to achieve her goal. Nothing was able to stop her drive for success—for her, failure was not an option. If, in the future, she remains true to her determination, then her star is just beginning to ascend, and her fans will reap the benefit of more amazing country music. And for Crystal, her fame brought an extra bonus: When she performed at the Grand Ole Opry, just as her grandfather had predicted she would, he was able to watch her on TV just before he passed away.

Contact Crystal Shawanda
Website: www.crystalshawandaonline.com
To contact Crystal, sign up on the website.

Blackfire

PUNK ROCK AND TRADITIONAL NAVAJO

Are you ready for some true indigenous punk rock? If so, check out the Native American group Blackfire. Their music, exemplified by their 2008 double-disc CD, *Silence Is a Weapon,* is extraordinarily distinct. The album is like no other, with the first disc containing twelve turbocharged punk-rock songs and the second featuring traditional Diné (Navajo) music.

Blackfire members with their father, Jones Benally

Blackfire has the further distinction of being a family band. The three members of the band are siblings. Jeneda, the bass player, is the older sister of Clayson, the drummer, and Klee, the lead vocalist and guitarist. The three Benally siblings were born in a place called Big Mountain, in Black Mesa, Arizona. The area has long been a site of contention between the Native inhabitants and companies seeking to extract coal from the land. Since as long as they can remember, the Benally family has been involved with the many land struggles of the Diné, the name Navajo people use to refer to themselves and which translates into English as "the People."

When the children were young, they lived with their parents, Jones and Berta Benally, on the reservation. Because Jones was a medicine man and highly active in tribal affairs, the Benally children were steeped in Native culture and attended numerous tribal council meetings. However, their parents decided to move off the reservation and relocate to Flagstaff, Arizona, so the children could attend public school there.

Jeneda remembers, "When we became school age, we moved off the reservation because my parents did not want me to go to a boarding school. My father went to a boarding school, and they did not like the idea of shipping me off somewhere at such a young age and only seeing me on weekends." At the time, Klee was still very young, and Clayson was just a baby.

Although the family did not live on the reservation, they remained deeply connected to it. However, while Jeneda was still being imbued with Diné traditions through her family and Native elders, the public school was attempting to diminish or eliminate the influence of her Navajo culture. When she first started attending elementary school, in the 1980s in Flagstaff, she was part of a program aimed at ridding Navajo students of their Diné accent. The result, she says today, is that "now, I really have to work on my beautiful Diné accent that I miss so much."

When Jeneda was in the third grade, the family moved to the Grand Canyon area, where they would live for about six years. School there was much better for the Benally children, and they lived their lives as most normal kids would. Clayson remembers their continued connection to their Navajo culture and issues: "Every weekend or every chance we could get, our father was helping us to participate in ceremonies and pow-wows, even though we did not live on the reservation. We come from a place called Big Mountain, and we have always been involved with the different land struggles. We went to many meetings at our chapter houses and were involved in the political aspects of our tribal councils as well."

Given the influence of their Native upbringing, immersed as it was in singing and dancing, it wasn't long before Jeneda, Klee, and Clayson would begin to involve themselves in music. Jeneda remembers when she first began to play the instrument that she would ultimately play in Blackfire: "I started playing bass when I was thirteen years old. The bass was a lot bigger than I was, and in order to reach the end of the bass, I had to physically move it to hit those nice deep notes." Her brothers followed suit, with Klee picking up the guitar at about twelve years old and Clayson beginning to play the drums at ten.

For the most part, the Benally siblings did the best they could to teach themselves how to play. Because of the limited resources where they lived, they had few other options. Jeneda talks about their transition from traditional music to picking up modern instruments and playing contemporary music: "We do not view art as something separate from our life and our daily practices. It was just a natural progression for us to pick up these modern tools."

When Jeneda reached her sophomore year in high school, the entire family moved back to Flagstaff. Before the move, Jeneda had been excelling in school, maintaining a 4.0 grade-point average. When she attended her new high school in Flagstaff, she was overwhelmed by the amount of racism that existed. Jeneda remembers a profound culture shock: "When we moved back, I went from being a 4.0 student to wanting to drop out. There was a lot of racism. The way that non-Native people spoke about Natives was so degrading that it was hard to cope. It was shocking. Unfortunately, my brothers experienced not just emotional discrimination but physical violence as well."

At their junior high school, Klee and Clayson encountered racial slander and sometimes attacks to the point of having to defend themselves. In one instance, fellow classmates injured Clayson. "We had thick accents and long hair when we were younger," he remembers. "In junior high, people held me down against my will and held a lighter flame to my stomach and scarred me. It is something that I carry and live with today. I know many other Native kids that come off the reservation have to go to school here and continue to face these realities." Fortunately, Clayson and Klee later transferred to a desirable charter school.

And, after only half a semester, Jeneda also was thankful to be able to change schools. Her new school, Verde Valley High School, based its entire value system on learning about other cultures and embracing a global community. Not only did her grades pick up, but she also was able to obtain a bass teacher, although the experience was not exactly what she had hoped it would be. Jeneda recalls, "Verde Valley High School was fantastic. I had tried to teach myself bass and it was a little bit difficult. The school said, 'We can find you a bass teacher.' They did, and I had a great bass teacher, but the problem was that we talked about philosophy and how we could make positive changes in the world, which is great, but we did not play as much bass as talk philosophy."

Not getting to play the bass as much as she would have liked in school did not keep Jeneda from practicing at home with her brothers. Klee remembers the early start of their musical group: "We had been a living-room band for quite some time. We were playing and practicing. We did not know anybody else's songs, because we were just still learning our instruments. We were just making up our own songs."

They had each chosen their instruments, and as Klee describes it, "These instruments helped us to create songs."

Klee Benally, lead vocalist and guitarist for Blackfire, never holds back during a performance.

Yet it was not just the instruments that molded their songs but also the "stuff" of their lives. In those early days, the musical siblings who would evolve into the band Blackfire established the essence of their music. Their songs, Klee says, are "about modern history and things that we want to bring attention to, especially to the youth, because of the injustices we have experienced. When you see injustices happening, you can get angry about it, but what you do with that anger is the difference. We turn that angry energy into creating something positive. We channel it into our art. We sing about it and express what is going on for people to gain a better understanding and insight."

By 1989, Jeneda, Clayson, and Klee had made significant progress since their early days of practicing, and they were excited when some of their mother's friends were playing at a New Year's Eve event and asked the siblings if they would like to start the show with a couple of songs. Jeneda remembers, "Oh, my gosh, were we scared. We debated about it and asked each other, 'Should we do it? Should we do it?'" Two songs were all they knew, but they decided to give it a shot.

According to Jeneda, the crowd went wild after their performance, clapping and screaming. On that New Year's Eve, on the cusp of 1990, Blackfire was truly born. Within a short time of that life-changing performance, the band was asked to perform at several local venues. Their second show was performed for the American Indian Science and Engineering Group in the Prochnow Auditorium at Northern Arizona University in Flagstaff. Thinking back, Clayson says, "That was a big crowd. It was scary. I think I was eleven or twelve. I ended up doing a drum solo."

The siblings began to play at schools and residences throughout their community and back on the reservation. Recalling those early days of Blackfire, Clayson says, "It was such an amazing experience to be in front of your peers to express your creative insights. It really shaped a lot of our messages and the direction that we wanted to go. We wanted to see positive change and affect things in a positive way to help our families, relatives, and neighbors."

Within a short time, Blackfire was performing at venues all over Arizona. The punk-rock scene was flourishing at the time, both locally and internationally, and Blackfire began performing with other punk bands such as the Vandals, a California group. Blackfire really connected with the music of punk bands like the Ramones, a New York group often regarded as the first punk rockers; Dead Kennedys, from the San Francisco scene; and Midnight Oil, from Australia. In describing his passion for these bands' creative expression as "something more than the superficial music that we heard on the radio," Klee says, "It had that type of honest energy that addressed anger and frustration but in a way that was not just about hatred or complete negativity; it was about releasing that energy." Because they had witnessed and experienced social and environmental injustice in their community, Blackfire found punk rock to be a natural outlet for their creative expression as well. It allowed them to transform their anger into something positive. "Through expressing our concerns and communicating them," says Klee, "we can hope it will inspire people to take action. They can recognize that these issues are ongoing and that something can be done about them."

WHERE DID THE NAME BLACKFIRE COME FROM?

Big Mountain is a site located in Black Mesa. Black Mesa is the ancestral home of the Benally family and serves as the inspiration for Blackfire's name. Since 1960, coal-mining operations have harvested vast deposits of coal on these sacred Diné (Navajo) lands. Continuous fires have burned because of these operations, causing pollution in the form of thick, black smoke. This is where the group derived their name, Blackfire.

According to Blackfire, the pollution from these mining operations has contributed to the forced relocation of more than 14,000 Diné people from their ancestral homelands. After choosing the name for their group, the members learned that "Blackfire" in the Diné language, *Kótizhiní*, literally translates as "fire-black." This was a term from Diné warrior societies meaning "the enemy is approaching," an event warriors communicated by placing a blanket over a fire, resulting in plumes of dark, black smoke.

While they were playing their own music, the members of Blackfire never missed an opportunity to enjoy a performance by other artists and bands in their genre. The one concert Jeneda went to that not only inspired her but also resulted in a career-changing event was the Ramones. After the concert, she told a girlfriend she was "so floored" by the band that she was ready to follow them to their next concert, which was in Austin, Texas. The two drove there together, arriving just in time for the show. Jeneda had written a note to the band, believing they were a family band because of their shared last name of Ramone. C. J. Ramone contacted her after the concert, saying, "I'm sorry to tell you, but we are not a family band." Although their stage names all ended in Ramone, none of the band members were actually related. However, Jeneda and C. J., as she puts it, "really connected on a deep level. C. J. and I were like long-lost siblings; he has been part of our family ever since."

Soon after their meeting, Jeneda introduced C. J. to Blackfire's music. As a result, C. J. offered to produce their first album. They got to work and produced a five-song CD. The production company distributed the album worldwide, and because of this widespread distribution, a French journalist obtained a copy. He called the band members to arrange an interview, then flew to the United States and followed Blackfire for a week, conducting interviews and taking photos. Subsequently, a prominent French magazine featured Blackfire on its cover. Soon after the magazine hit the stands, concert promoters invited Blackfire to tour in Europe.

Between tours, Blackfire continued to put out more music. In 1998, they self-produced an EP, a three-song, self-titled album. They were involved in numerous compilation albums with other punk artists and independently released their first full-length CD, *One Nation Under*, featuring Joey Ramone on two songs and also Jones Benally. This raw-energy album scored Blackfire the Nammy for Best Pop/Rock Recording at the 2002 Native American Music Awards.

Their European tour led to international tours and memorable experiences. Perhaps the most unforgettable was a concert in Germany, where a Tuareg band named Tinariwen was also playing. The Tuaregs are a desert tribe from the Sahara Desert in Africa, and the band did not speak English. Yet, according to Jeneda, the two groups were able to communicate through music. Jeneda remembers the awesome experience: "We played back to back with Tinariwen. The emotion and energy of their music was our translator. There was a profound connection." Tinariwen was organizing a musical festival in the Sahara, and they hoped that Blackfire would be able to come and play.

After their European tour, a promoter with no connection to Tinariwen wrote to invite Blackfire to the 2003 Festival of the Desert, a gathering that showcases traditional Tuareg

WHAT IS AN EP?

An EP album, short for "extended play album," is a CD that contains more than just a single song but not enough songs to qualify as an LP, or long play album. EPs are generally fifteen to twenty-eight minutes long, while an LP is anywhere from thirty to nearly eighty minutes long.

In the 1950s and 1960s, EPs were released as "album samplers," that is, snippets of a larger album as a marketing enticement. These albums were released on small, seven-inch black vinyl records with two songs on each side and were made to be played on a record player—a far cry from downloading a song to an MP3 player.

music as well as music from around the world. Jeneda, Klee, and Clayson were thrilled to attend the concert, held in Essakane, Mali, a country in the Sahara Desert. The concert not only reunited them with their friends, the band members of Tinariwen, but also gave them the opportunity to perform with such internationally accomplished musicians as the Malian ensemble Tartit; Malians Ali Farka Touré and Oumou Sangaré; the French-based world musicians Lo'Jo; Django; and Robert Plant with Afro-beat and roots guitarist Justin Adams.

Back in the United States, Blackfire released an album titled *Woody Guthrie Singles* in 2004. It features music they wrote for two previously unreleased and unpublished Woody Guthrie lyrics. Woody Guthrie is a renowned folk singer and songwriter whose most well-known song is "This Land Is Your Land." Later that year, Blackfire went back to the Sahara to perform at the 2004 Festival in the Desert. After their return, they were the first Native American group ever invited to play on the Warped Tour. Afterward, they produced *Blackfire—Beyond Warped: Live Music Series*, a dual-disc CD/DVD. To the group's amazement, in 2005 *Woody Guthrie Singles* earned them the nomination and Nammy for Group of the Year at the Native American Music Awards.

Blackfire continued to tour in the United States and around the world. In 2007, they began working on *Silence Is a Weapon*, their double-disc CD featuring both their energetic punk-rock and traditional Navajo music. The group was once again thrilled with the recognition given to their musicianship by the Native American Music Awards. *Silence Is a Weapon* garnered the 2008 Nammy for Record of the Year, and the album's producer, Ed Stasiam, won the Native Heart, a special award that recognizes significant contributions of non-Natives to Native American music.

On the one hand, Klee describes winning awards as great, saying, "It is always good to be recognized by your peers or other people in the Native music community. I remember a time when almost all of the Native musicians knew each other. Now there are many more, and it is great to see how people are being encouraged to recognize them in these ways." On the other hand, Klee clarifies that winning awards does not motivate him to make music. Rather, he is motivated by music's ability to be an educational vehicle. He is interested in facilitating awareness of issues to create some sort of social transformation. He describes *Silence Is a Weapon* as an album that "expresses the need for people to speak out and to take action in times of silence or fear." He adds, "To be recognized is a good thing because it means that somebody is listening."

Jeneda's feelings about being an award-winning musician are much the same. She admits she is honored and inspired by the recognition given to the band by their peers: "We don't do this for awards, but it is nice to be recognized for the work that we do. I think it's always nice when socially conscious music or a positive message gets recognition. I

Album cover for *Silence Is a Weapon*

think there needs to be positive change in our communities. I am grateful."

Since 1989, wherever they have played—in the United States, Canada, Mexico, several European countries, and even the Sahara Desert in Mali, Africa—Blackfire has been turning on audiences with its politically charged, alternative-style punk-rock music. In addition, with the help of their father, Jones Benally, they have introduced traditional Diné dance and music to the crowds that come to watch their shows. The band refuses to play in anything other than all-age venues, meaning people of any age can attend their shows. They also believe in and promote the principle of staying away from drugs and alcohol.

Clayson feels that what Blackfire does is unique. He says they provide not just entertainment but also a form of education that addresses a great need for people to gain understanding and break down stereotypes and myths. Traveling throughout the world has taught him how small the world really is: "To share, to connect with other communities, and to bring some of that awareness to indigenous people is an amazing opportunity with which we are blessed." And he knows that Blackfire's work is not done, that it must keep moving forward, because "we have brothers and sisters in all of these different indigenous communities throughout the world."

Jeneda agrees that being able to travel and share who they are with so much of the world has been a blessing: "This is how we build bridges to break down the concepts of intolerance and hate." She loves and values cultural diversity so much that when she was in Mali she wore only traditional clothing. She explains why: "I always try to blend in and dress traditionally. I do not want to influence anyone's culture with any sort of my own Western influence. Their culture is valuable, and I have seen what Western culture has done to mine."

Jeneda hopes that people who hear Blackfire's music are inspired to learn about their own cultural heritage. Believing that the basis of all traditional cultures is respect—respect for our families, our communities, our environments, and ourselves—she hopes that Blackfire and its music inspire people to learn this very important and basic value. She has seen the changes the band can make in reaching their audiences by empowering them to discover their identities. When kids come to their shows, the band asks them what clan they're from and what their heritage is, and the response is often "I don't know." But a seed has been planted. The kids go home and find out what their cultural heritage is, and when they return for the next show, they are so proud and excited to be able tell the band who they are. Jeneda says, "Young people are learning their culture, and to me that is one of our most amazing accomplishments."

The members of Blackfire express their strong ethics when offering their advice about becoming a musician, advice that is equally applicable to any path in life. According to Jeneda, "Life is a lesson, and I think throughout life we need to remember that every day we should learn something new." She always keeps in mind that her decisions and the decisions of her siblings will influence future generations. For that reason, they let kids know that the band draws its strength from its culture and identity and that everything they do, they do without drugs and alcohol. She states emphatically, "You do not need drugs or alcohol to be in the music scene."

Klee emphasizes the power of perseverance and the freedom to make mistakes, as long those mistakes become learning experiences. He also addresses the potential conflict between the traditional world and the modern world: "We sometimes view them as antagonistic or separate, but what helped me since I was young is something that our father taught us—there is just one world crossed by different paths. We can still maintain and sustain our cultural heritage and walk in this modern world."

Clayson states that Blackfire has maintained its independence for the sake of integrity. He says they are fortunate to have their traditional culture, because it is what has given them their morals and values, the foundation they need to face their challenges. He believes that it does not matter what field a person chooses to go into, those challenges will always be there. His advice is to "maintain who you are, maintain a good sense of direction, and always do your best. You should always have integrity."

Addressing the reality of working in the music industry, what Clayson calls "trying to make a living on your creative expression," he says that Blackfire approaches songwriting by speaking from their hearts to represent what they know. He, like Klee, emphasizes perseverance and also thinking outside the box, "especially as an indigenous person. There are many challenges to indigenous musicians. People will want you to play into the stereotype, and you just have to know who you are and always remain honest."

Blackfire has begun work on an acoustic album, which is scheduled for release in 2009. In 2010, this powerful family band will have been performing for twenty years. Perhaps no group has done more through music to fight for indigenous rights and give a voice to Native American people. In addition,

Clayson Benally, Blackfire's drummer, is also an award-winning hoop dancer.

DID YOU KNOW? OTHER FACTS ABOUT MEMBERS OF THE GROUP BLACKFIRE

Jeneda Benally not only plays bass for Blackfire, but she is also a well-regarded storyteller, artist, and jewelry maker. She has held the title of Miss Flagstaff Indian Days Powwow Princess. She is also a national Native American Honor Roll Society member and a spokesperson for the Navajo Nation Tribal Employee Program.

Klee Benally, lead vocalist and guitarist for Blackfire, formed the Indigenous Action Media Group to offer filmmaking opportunities to Native American youth. He was also the winner of Best in Show at the Navajo Show at the Museum of Northern Arizona in 1991. It was the first time in the museum's sixty-four-year history that a student won the award for a Diné (Navajo) style bag made without the use of metal.

Clayson Benally, Blackfire's drummer, is a traditional storyteller, an award-winning Hoop Dancer, and a Northern Traditional Dancer. He has been lecturing at colleges since he was a teenager and is an accomplished artist and silversmith.

perhaps no group has so beautifully and so successfully combined traditional and contemporary music. Nevertheless, one thing is for sure: Blackfire will continue to create high-energy alternative music and inspire other Native American musicians to do the same.

Contact Blackfire
P.O. Box 1492
Flagstaff, AZ 86002
Website: www.blackfire.net
To contact Blackfire, sign up on the website.

Leela Gilday

VOCALIST AND COMPOSER WITH A MESSAGE OF HOPE AND EMPOWERMENT

Leela Gilday, Dené performing artist, not only sings beautifully but also writes beautiful songs. Her songs are wonderful music as well as messages of hope, strength, and empowerment. Leela consciously chose this path for her music, hoping to fill the void created by the lack of Native women's voices in the music of her youth. Today she is a multi-award-winning folk artist, representing the voice that was missing when she was growing up.

Leela Gilday

Leela was born in 1974, in Yellowknife, in the Northwest Territories of Canada, a vast area containing a large concentration of Native people, almost 50 percent of them members of the five main groups of Dené. Growing up in the Northwest Territories, Leela experienced relatively little prejudice. In fact, the opposite was true. Leela explains, "Dené hold many of the positions of power in the Northwest Territories. We have had a couple of Dené premiers, and Dené people hold many of the key government positions. A long-time national representative in the House of Commons was Dené. I grew up in a culture that emphasized the power of the Dené and our rights to the land."

In addition to Leela's strong cultural upbringing, she also had a happy family life. Her parents, Cindy Kenny-Gilday and Bill Gilday, were close and raised Leela in a positive and loving environment. In fact, they are still together and recently celebrated their thirty-fifth wedding anniversary. Leela says that it was music that brought her parents together: "My dad was a trombone player. He was just a young dude in Ontario who had his own music studio. He taught from his studio, and he played in big bands and swing bands to make his living." When Bill met Cindy in the North, he asked her father, Leela's grandfather, for permission to marry her. "My grandfather said, 'Well, you can marry my daughter, but you can't take her out of the North,' and my dad said, 'Okay, that's a great deal.'"

At the time her parents married, there was not much work for a trombone player in Yellowknife. Consequently, Leela's father obtained work as a music teacher at the local school in Yellowknife. In fact, Leela's father was her music teacher from second grade to sixth grade. She remembers it as a basically good experience, except when a schoolmate didn't like him. Then it could be troublesome.

The Gilday family included three children: Leela and her brother and sister, Jay and Carla Gilday. Because of their mother and father's love for music, singing and dancing was a large and integral part of their childhood. Leela loved to sing, and at the age of eight, she performed her first gig at Yellowknife Folk on the Rocks Fall Festival, with her dad accompanying her on the piano. This was the start of her singing career, and performances in other venues followed, such as at Dené Tea Dance ceremonies and community gatherings and dances.

Throughout elementary, junior high, and high school, Leela dabbled in all sorts of music, whether it was singing or dancing to music or learning a musical instrument. She learned to play the trumpet in seventh grade, and even attempted to learn a few notes on the trombone, the instrument her father played. Leela was becoming so involved with singing that when she was in the eighth grade, the entire family moved to Toronto for one year so that she could sing with the Toronto Children's Chorus, the most prestigious children's choir in Canada. The following year, the family moved back to Yellowknife, and Leela continued her education through high school.

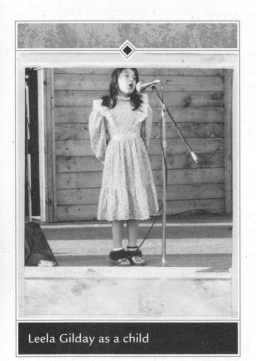

Leela Gilday as a child

In addition to singing and playing musical instruments, Leela also wrote song lyrics. She laughs when remembering the songs that she wrote during her high school years. "They were just terrible love and broken-heart songs," recalls Leela. Although she pokes fun at the music she wrote as a teenager, her early songwriting helped prepare her to become the musician that she is today.

It's no surprise, then, that given all the different aspects of music surrounding her all her life, Leela decided, at age seventeen, to study music at the University of Alberta-Edmonton. And she was not satisfied studying just general music; she went full force and decided to study classical opera, not an easy subject. Her courses included classical vocal training, classical composition, and musical performance.

Leela's first year at the university was a bit of an awakening. Although she was excited to dive into the world of music studies, she was unprepared for the discrimination she faced. She remembers specifically a time when a group of college boys in a limousine screamed racially derogatory terms at her. "The university in Edmonton is one of the most difficult areas in terms of racism. I did experience a lot of discrimination, especially being a young Native woman," she recalls.

Leela hung in and made it through her first year. During her sophomore year, she traveled to South America as part of her university study-through-service program, teaching English and drama to South American students. She also took part in several environmental cleanup projects. In her last two years at the university, after her return from South America, Leela struggled in some areas of classical instruction, namely classical composition. She recalls, "I was in my composition class, and I just knew I wasn't a classical composer. I really did not have the passion for it." Still, Leela pressed forward, excelling in other areas. She sang in multiple operas at the university, including singing the part of Marcellina in *The Marriage of Figaro* as a mezzo soprano.

Leela remembers some of the more intense moments of life at the university: "I was in the practice room for five hours every day, especially in my last two years. But so was everybody else who was in music school, right? You don't do well in music school unless you work for it." And work for it she did, and in spite of experiencing some difficulty, she finished her four-year course of instruction at the university.

After graduation, Leela decided to move to Toronto, Ontario, Canada's largest city. She got a job with the National Aboriginal Achievement Foundation, fully intending to return to school the following year to pursue a master's degree in classical performance. But her life took a detour, as life often does. She started playing the guitar, propelled by a feeling that something was missing from her life. Leela explains, "I was not hearing proper women's voices or proper Native voices represented in the music I was singing. That really weighed on me. I really needed to write songs that represented those things within me. That is why I went into songwriting."

Leela emphasizes that she did not jump right into a full-time musical career when she left the university. Even though she had been performing since she was young, had studied classical music, and had practiced singing four to five hours a day, she knew she needed to build up both her experience and her repertoire. She felt she had to pay her dues, because she had no sense of what it would actually take to get to the point of being able to perform her own songs. During this period of intense commitment to her music, she did not even own a television. Her energy was devoted to creating a repertoire of songs.

While pursuing her songwriting and performing ambitions, Leela held multiple daytime jobs. She worked for temp agencies, as a waitress, and at a television station. She even worked as a door-to-door salesperson selling counterfeit money detectors. She was willing to do whatever it took to succeed as a musician, as long as the work was honest and she was trying her best.

She started getting gigs at local establishments. She would do all the legwork for the performances, putting up posters and calling friends and acquaintances to attend the shows. Before the shows, she would carry and set up all her equipment. She played music wherever she could. She played at coffee houses and cafes. She even played at a goulash house, which, according to Leela, turned out to have a huge crowd.

. After six years, Leela felt that she had worked long and hard enough and had paid her dues to her satisfaction. She decided now was the time to put her songs—an eclectic mix of folk, pop, and traditional elements addressing love and the world—into an album. Her parents and her grandparents each kicked in about $2,000, and Leela paid the remaining $10,000. She worked with a talented producer for eight months to create her first CD, *Spirit World, Solid Wood*, which was released in March 2002.

. At twenty-six years old, Leela entered a new chapter in her life. Though she enjoyed living in Toronto, she decided to move back to Edmonton to be near her brother and sister. She was considering eventually moving back to Yellowknife in the Northwest Territories, saying, "I'm a Northern girl, and I needed to be next to the land." But before making that definitive move, she made a decision that would change the course of her life. Because she had just finished her CD, she decided to make a last grand effort to become a full-time musician. She found an apartment in Edmonton for $300 a month and loaded her car up with stacks of *Spirit World, Solid Wood*. This was the time for her, the time for her to try to make it. It was now or never. She recalls, "It was so crazy. I was educated; I had put in the time, paid my dues. I was twenty-six years old and I thought, 'If I am not going to be a full-time musician now, then it is not going to happen.' But you know what? It worked, and I never looked back. I sent out tons of promo packages, and I played anywhere that would have me."

. Leela's persistence paid off. She began getting work as a performer, and her CD started garnering radio airplay across Canada. Now, at last, she was gaining considerable respect as a musician. In 2002, she was nominated for Best Songwriter, Best Female Artist, and Best Folk Album for *Spirit World, Solid Wood* at the Fourth Annual Canadian Aboriginal Music Awards. Imagine Leela's elation when she won all three awards. Then, in 2003, she was nominated at the Juno Awards for Aboriginal Recording of the Year.

Leela then began to work on her second album, pouring her heart into it. In fact, she named it *Sedzé*, which translates as "my heart" in her native North Slavey language. She released the album on November 22, 2006, and it, too, was critically well received. In 2007, Leela was nominated for two Canadian Aboriginal Music Awards, for Best Album of the Year and Best Songwriter. She was also nominated for three Aboriginal Peoples Choice Music Awards, for Best Songwriter, Best Folk/Acoustic CD, and Aboriginal Entertainer of the Year.

Leela was thrilled to be nominated for such prestigious awards but was particularly excited when she was nominated for and won three different awards that same year— Best Folk Album at the Indian Summer Music Awards, Best Aboriginal Recording of the Year at the Western Canadian Music Awards, and Aboriginal Recording of the Year at the Juno Awards.

Leela says that being nominated for and then winning in three categories was really exciting for her, but that what she really values is the sense of community that these award shows create among Native musicians. At her many performances, whether at a festival, show, or musical gathering, she is often the only Native artist, so she finds it tremendously satisfying to go somewhere and be with a whole community of people who understand what it is to be a Native artist. Many of her closest friends are in that community. Leela says, "I am thankful for that sense of community. It has changed my career. I think it has given me a niche that allows me to build strength, build companions, and celebrate the strength of our contribution." Because pursuing music as a career is such a tough road, Leela sometimes finds herself feeling down and thinking, "Why am I doing this?" But she reminds herself that "what I have to offer is very valuable." She thinks it is very important that Native stories get told, and the artists—each one with a unique voice—are the ones responsible for telling them. She is very clear about it: "That is my job."

More than anything, Leela's thrilling win at the 2008 Juno Awards for Aboriginal Recording of the Year kicked her career into high gear. That award, together with the help of a new agent, propelled her into becoming a successful, independent touring musician. She began performing at much more respectable venues all over Canada and even in Japan, tripling the amount of money she and her musicians had been making. Her naturally powerful voice and heartfelt

Leela Gilday

songs have earned her fans all across Canada and even worldwide. She has been featured in numerous magazines and newspapers, including *Up Here* magazine, in which she was named 2007 Northerner of the Year, and has appeared on CBC and APTN (Aboriginal Peoples Television Network). In 2008, Leela was featured in a music video, "One Drum," presented at the Fargo Film Festival in North Dakota. The video won an Honorable Mention Award.

Leela is happy with her life right now and has no regrets about her decision to pursue her own brand of music. She gets to travel, has performed for thousands of people, and plays with, in her own words, some "amazing musicians" in some "perfect shows." In addition, she conducts workshops on songwriting and voice empowerment and serves as a role model. She credits her success to total commitment and hard work. She does not even believe in having a backup plan, believing instead that if you prepare yourself, that if you have a dream and it is your path, that "things will happen that you never expect will happen. It is just music; it is just life, and if you fail, you can get up and try again. If you really do not want to do it, then you will figure out the back-up plan when it comes to that. But if you go in expecting to fail, then you will fail. It is a self-fulfilling prophecy."

Tough as an artist's life can be, it also has its amazing qualities, those moments that redeem the hard times. These are what Leela focuses on. She tells two stories to illustrate. A few years ago, she was having a terrible time. She was sick and nothing was going right. She was fighting with her guitar player and performing low-energy shows. Worst of all, the audiences were not responding the way she wanted them to. One day after a show, when she was packing up her gear and feeling depressed, Leela was approached by a young woman who was carrying one child and pushing another in a stroller. The woman reached out her hand and gave Leela a beautiful silver-and-turquoise bracelet. Leela asked, "What is this for?" and the woman responded, "You know, Leela, it is to say thank you, because your music has helped me through my breakup, it has helped me be strong for my kids, and it has made all the difference in the world to me." Leela was blown away and realized right then and there that not only were things not so bad but also that the gift giver's response to her music was the reason why she was a musician: "My music is medicine beyond the reference of myself—it is not in front of me; it comes through me."

Leela also recounts another touching experience, which occurred on June 21, 2008, Aboriginal Day in Canada. Leela was on APTN performing in her hometown of Yellowknife. She was there with her band, looking great, and in front of the stage were about fifteen little girls, all with their hands on the stage looking up at her, just smiling away. After the performance, they came up to her and asked for autographs. Leela thought, "This is the reason I do this, because these kids can know that no matter where you come from or what you are, you've got to believe in yourself and you've got to do what's right for your heart." She knew that, for the girls, seeing a successful Dené woman is like seeing themselves grown up and realizing that success is possible. And Leela knows that it is not only really cool for the girls but that it is also cool for her, "because I think it takes me out of myself and my own issues, because it is not really about me, right?"

By her bedside, Leela keeps a quote from Johann Wolfgang von Goethe, a German poet and dramatist, which she looks at often for inspiration. Leela's philosophy is illustrated so well in the last line of the quote: "Whatever you can do, or dream you can do, begin it. Boldness has genius, power, and magic in it. Begin it now." Leela was fortunate. As she says, "I was one of those people who knew what she wanted to do from a young age." Her rise from a young girl immersed in music to one of Canada's better-known performing artists and major vocalists inspires not just young girls but all people who want to do something extraordinary with their lives. Leela Gilday studied hard, worked hard, made a commitment, and achieved her highest dream.

Contact Leela Gilday
Website: www.leelagilday.com
To contact Leela, sign up on the website.

Four Rivers Drum

POWWOW DRUM GROUP

For many Native Americans and Aboriginal First Nations people, powwows are an integral part of growing up. These gatherings are both ceremonies and celebrations, times for singing and dancing, for renewing old friendships and making new ones. Organized drum groups are the music makers at powwows. Without their drumming there would be no singing, and without the singing there would be no dancing. The drum groups play a

Four Rivers Drum

powerful role in preserving the essence of the rich and varied Native heritages and cultures.

Every drum group has a lead singer and a second singer who repeats the leader's line in a similar or different range. The songs played by drum groups vary widely, ranging from traditional to modern, and may be sung in English, in the song's original Native language, or in the language of one of the group's members. Drum styles also vary—there are Northern and Southern styles—to accommodate the different types of dances that are performed at powwows.

The drum group generally performs around the edge of the dance circle. When more than one drum group is present at a powwow, the groups take turns playing, and, often, certain groups will play requested songs. Most drummers are men, although there are some women drummers and even a few all-women drum groups. More often, the women stand around the outside of the circle and sing.

People gravitate toward the drum groups, and crowds gather around while they play. The most popular groups receive multiple requests to perform at powwows, and some have gained national stature. Canyon Records, a Native American record company, has recorded several drum groups that have created very popular albums of traditional drum music.

Four Rivers Drum is an outstanding example of a vibrant drum group. The group started with four drummers and singers in the mid-1990s and quickly grew to ten drummers from six different tribal nations. The group played at their first five powwows without a name; in fact, locals referred to them as the No Name Drum. In time, they came up with the name Four Rivers Drum. The name refers to their location on the peninsula in the tidewater area of Virginia, where the cities of Chesapeake, Hampton, Newport News, Norfolk, Portsmouth, Virginia Beach, and Williamsburg are located. Whenever the group travels to a powwow, they must cross any one of four rivers that surround them.

By January 2009, Four Rivers Drum had grown to nineteen members, comprising ten drummers and nine singers. The group also includes a spiritual elder of the drum, Martha Spencer. Members come from diverse backgrounds, yet express themselves similarly when it comes to their heartfelt ties to the group. Following are descriptions of those ties— how they came to be and why they are so valued—by the majority of Four Rivers Drum's current members.

The husband and wife team of Bob Jondreau and Jamie Ware-Jondreau is a big part of the group. Bob, an Ojibwa (also known as Chippewa) Indian, is from the Keweenaw Bay Indian Community near Lake Superior in northwestern Michigan. He has been involved with Four Rivers Drum since its inception, is the leader and keeper of the drum, and also is the overseer of the group.

Bob stayed in his community until he was seventeen. He and his family faced extensive racism, and he finds that racism, prejudice, and discrimination are still "alive and well" across the country: "I've been told to get my rear end off the street in a racially derogatory way, and I have been called terribly racist names." Today, he tries to learn from his encounters with prejudice and tells his family to do the same.

Jamie Ware-Jondreau, a member of the Rappahannock Tribe, which was part of the Powhatan Confederacy, is a singer in the group. Although there is a Rappahannock County in Virginia, the tribe itself does not have a reservation, and Jamie was raised in the Hampton Roads area of Virginia. The Jondreaus have a daughter, Meno, who spends a lot of time with the group during practices and performances.

The Jondreau family loves what the drum represents, and they love the close ties the members of the group experience by being in Four Rivers Drum. Bob explains, "I love the people. I love the way the drum has brought people together from all walks of life. The drum does not care if the people are recovering from anything; as long as they remain fighting their ghosts, they are welcomed to the drum." In the last fourteen years, he has had to ask only one individual who encircled the drum to leave. He says, "When anyone feels that he or she is bigger than the drum, he or she is no longer needed."

Everyone involved in Four Rivers Drum values its connection to Indian heritage, and the Jondreau family is no different. Bob's favorite aspect of the group is the process of discovery it brings. He says, "I love the look of the drummers' or singers' faces lighting up when we've practiced hard to get a song down, or their reaction when the song makes the drum dance and the dancers come back and say 'good tone' or 'good song.'"

Bob is optimistic about the direction of Four Rivers Drum and its growth. His enthusiasm was not even dampened when the Queen of England herself cancelled an appearance at a Jamestown celebration where Four Rivers Drum played. He knows there are bigger things to come: "Where the drum goes from here is up to the folks who drum and sing. When the drum is ready, we will know where we are going."

Michael Cloud-Butler, advisor to the younger members of Four Rivers Drum, is an enrolled member of the Lake Superior Band of Chippewa Indians, also known as Anishinaabeg and Ojibwa, in Wisconsin. Since the 1990s, he has been a close friend of Bob Jondreau, the group's drum keeper, and has been a member of Four Rivers Drum since the beginning of 2007.

Because Michael has extensive experience with Native American drums, he takes care to share his knowledge of the history of the traditional ways of the drum with newer members. He teaches them older traditional songs approved for all drum groups and has plans to compose and teach new songs for the drum that will be unique to the group.

Michael honors the drum as a revered object having a life of its own, explaining that "Indian drums have a great air of sacredness about them; they are focal points of the sacred aspect of the Creation." He has seen drums in all shapes, sizes, and colors, in various states of repair and made of dif-

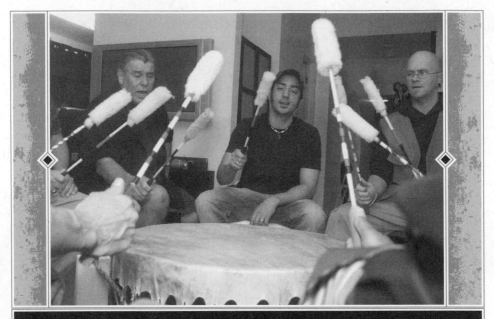

Author Vincent Schilling (center) was asked by Michael Cloud-Butler (left) to play with Four Rivers Drum.

ferent materials. He saw one that was simply a marching-band drum with one side removed and propped on a stack of blankets. But he says that every drum "should be honored and respected for being our voice to the Spirits and Gitchie Manito [Great Spirit]; it is the vehicle by which we express our small understanding of the Creation and tell the Creator that we remember him and what he teaches us." The beliefs held by Indians that the drum is a symbol of the earth itself, that its sound binds people to the "heartbeat of Mother Earth," and that the voices of the men and women around it "play into the rhythm of everything surrounding us" are sacred truths that Michael fully believes. He also believes that the drum has a healing quality whose source is both in the hearts of the people around it and "the one who lives within the drum."

Throughout his life, Michael has experienced more than his share of racial prejudice. He characterizes the racism that he has encountered as "embedded everywhere in the American culture." It runs the gamut from overt instances of direct racist name calling—chief, injun, redskin, dog, dirty Hawaiian—to racially charged remarks thrown out casually but not aimed directly—drunken Indian, savage, too many chiefs. The majority of the prejudice Michael has experienced occurred not on his home reservation but in Virginia. He recalls one drunken individual saying to his face, "It's too bad Custer ran out of bullets," and another wisecracking, "Hey, Geronimo wants to talk to you!" But Michael shrugs off these hateful encounters and derogatory comments. Rather, he chooses to invest in the happier things in life, and his positive outlook and gentle spirit show it. He turns to the group Four Rivers Drum as a positive source: "For those moments that we sit together, I hear the members talking, laughing, and singing. We progress among ourselves as a family, with the faults built in, of course."

Sylvia Nery Strickland has been a singer with Four Rivers Drum since 2007. She was born and raised in Norfolk, Virginia, and eventually moved to Virginia Beach. Part Cherokee and part Filipino, Sylvia has experienced racism and discrimination since childhood, when she was the only person of color throughout her school years until high school. If there were other Indians in her school, says Sylvia, "no one dared claim it." Familiar with black, white, and Indian as basic racial categories, her schoolmates labeled her with the term "half-breed" and, occasionally, "dirty Jap." Her mother and grandmother told her never to tell anyone they were Indian. Her grandmother's words were, "They do not like Indians around here." In fact, because of her race, Sylvia could not sit at the lunch counter in Woolworth's (a former five-and-dime retail store chain) to get a soda. Her mother, who looked and passed as white, would buy one and pass it back to Sylvia, who stood and drank it.

Something in Sylvia as a young girl could not allow this denial of her identity. She once caused a family uproar that stemmed from one of her school-picture days that was also, coincidentally, a March of Dimes day. After donating her dime, she let her teacher pin a little red feather to her blouse. Sylvia describes what happened next: "When it was my picture time, I took the feather, stuck it straight up in my hair, and said I was ready." She can still remember the look of horror on the photographer's face as his assistant said, "Don't you want to take the feather from your hair? You look like an Indian." To which Sylvia replied, in no uncertain terms, "I am an Indian." When the assistant attempted to lay the feather flat, Sylvia stuck out her "fat lip" and said, "No, leave it alone!" She did not mention the incident to her parents, and when she proudly brought the pictures home and showed them to her parents, her mother almost fainted. Yet, in spite of her parents' displeasure over the picture, in retrospect Sylvia thinks they were probably somewhat proud of the strength and pride they had instilled in her. She learned later she would need this type of strength and pride to make it as, what she calls, a "mixed breed." In fact, some of Sylvia's most emotionally painful moments were instances of "real" reservation Indians being prejudiced toward her as a person of only partial heritage.

As difficult as aspects of Sylvia's life have been, she has found refuge in the fellowship of Four Rivers Drum. She enjoys not just the music the group creates but also the friendship. The ring tone on her cell phone is the song "Half-Breed." However, the term loses some of its power thanks to the mixture of lineages, cultures, and colors among Four Rivers Drum—Sylvia calls the group "a true level playing field that is diverse in every way." She thinks they all come to drum practice not just for the music but to be renewed. No matter how tired they are when they arrive, by the end of practice they are rejuvenated and full of life. For her personally, "it is a renewal, rebirth, and healing each week." She watches the faces of the drummers and can see "the absolute joy and energy in their faces" as the cares of the day and week melt away. She believes that, "While around our drum, we are one and we are there for the right reasons. What beautiful Spirits we have around our drum, those seen and those unseen."

Another singer in the group who is of mixed heritage is Jane Price. She is Swedish and Northern Cheyenne but is quick to assert that she surely favors the Indian mother she never knew. Jane was born in Crow Agency, Montana, the capital city of the Crow Tribe. She was adopted and later lived in the Lake Chautauqua area near Buffalo, New York. Chautauqua translates from its Indian language as "bag tied in the middle," and according to Jane, "The beauty there cannot be put into words." It is a place of mountains, lakes, streams, and winding dirt roads, thick with trees and wildflowers. She describes how she used to have "favorite places to go for every time of the year and for every emotion I was feeling. I miss having that."

In 2007, Jane was transferred through her work to a restaurant in Strawbridge, Virginia. From the beginning of her transfer, she was, as she describes it, "keenly aware that I had been sent there to cross paths with someone." Although she had previously met many people who had greatly enriched her life, the minute she met Michael Cloud-Butler and Sylvia Nery Strickland, she knew. She says, "The time we spent together was never enough." They invited her to join Four Rivers Drum, but it was not until the summer of 2008 that Jane's situation allowed her to accept their offer. Now she says that Michael, Sylvia, and every member of Four Rivers "have filled a hole in my spirit that I had been searching to fill for a very long time."

At the expense of sounding like a flower child, Jane says, "All the right auras are mixing together." She believes the members of Four Rivers Drum are on the right path together, that whatever lies ahead for them will be right, and she will welcome it with open arms. She gathers strength from them when they sing, laugh, and share opinions—it is a strength that cannot be compared to anything she has felt before, except for the feeling she gets from being with her immediate family. She says, in fact, "This is what I consider us: family. A door has opened because the right key was found, and I will be forever grateful."

Jane's gratitude is tempered by her awareness of people's continued preconceived notions and ignorance about Native Americans. As a food-industry employee, she interacts with a great number of people from all different backgrounds. Most of them want to know about her heritage, and she is always proud to share. During a conversation with an elderly couple who were fascinated with her Indian heritage, the discussion turned to another passion of hers, food, and then, specifically, to garlic. After she agreed with them that garlic was indeed the staff of life, the wife, quite astonished, looked at Jane and replied, "I didn't know your people ate garlic!" Jane's thought was, "What are we, vampires?" and she almost replied, "We enjoy sunshine too." She had to bite her cheeks to keep from doubling over in laughter before she excused herself. "But I laughed for the rest of that day and still find it amusing," she shares.

Anita and Hugh Harrell have been involved with Four Rivers Drum for over a year. Anita, a singer with the group, is of Shoshoni and Cherokee descent, while Hugh, a drummer, descends from the Chickahominy, Pamunkey, and Mattaponi Tribes. All three tribes are based in Virginia, and the latter two were part of the Powhatan Confederacy. Hugh grew up in Hampton, Virginia.

Anita has a true urban background, having grown up in Brooklyn, New York. She discloses that because she physically favors her African American heritage, she often experiences racism when she claims her Native American descent. She finds that people usually will assume that she and Hugh are either lying about their Native heritage or trying to be something other than African Americans. To illustrate, she tells the story of being at a reception for Chief

Wilma Mankiller after she spoke at a local university. A woman there noticed Anita's Native American–style choker and asked a bit condescendingly if she were Native. When Anita replied that she was, the woman asked her what tribe she was from. Anita gave her usual answer, that her mother was Shoshoni and her father Cherokee. The woman, with raised eyebrows, commented skeptically what an unusual combination that was, geographically speaking, and asked how her parents met. When Anita replied that they were both working in Manhattan, the woman exclaimed, "Good heavens, how on earth did they get there?" That gave Anita the perfect opportunity to answer with a deadpan look—and the truth. "By train," she said, and as she walked away, Anita heard a surprised gasp.

Her experience as a member of Four Rivers Drum is a completely different story. With the group, Anita feels nothing but friendship and cultural connection. She finds them welcoming, warm, and willing to share their knowledge of Native culture with those whom Anita describes as having become "acculturated into the larger society's mainly Europeanized focus. So long as we are willing to learn and put in the time, they are willing to teach." Both Anita and Hugh love this opportunity to reconnect with their Indian heritage, if not precisely the cultures of their specific ancestors. In addition, they feel that Four Rivers Drum has the potential to grow and become what Anita hopes will be "a first-rate drum group, recognized and requested frequently for its clean and powerful drumming and singing. That would be exciting and gratifying."

Both Four Rivers drummer Christopher Talyn Strum and singer Christina H. Carlson were born and raised in the Hampton Roads area and have lived there their entire lives. Talyn is a combination of Scotch-Irish, German, and Cherokee; Christina is German, Scotch-English, and Dakota. Because both have light complexions, they are often criticized for claiming any Native heritage. Talyn says that although he has "encountered some feelings that I am misappropriating Native culture," he has also encountered prejudice, to the point of losing a job, because of his appearance. He, as he put it, "answered a long-standing call from my spirit" and stretched his earlobes and wears a warrior's braid. The result is often trite and sarcastic ribbing, usually accompanied by pointing and snickering: "Did that hurt?" or "Are you in a gang?" or, sarcastically, "Cool haircut!" Talyn sees these moments as opportunities to inform and educate individuals about his decisions and what they mean to him, even though his response often changes the tone of the conversations in a negative way. Talyn says that "both Christina and I have noticed that when we mention being part Native, people's attitudes tend to change and certain assumptions are made, whether they are voiced or not."

Though their complexions may be light and their involvement with Four Rivers Drum recent, since 2008, the love Talyn and Christina share with other members of the group is deep reaching. They love not only the companionship and feeling of family but also the opportunity to learn from the elders through the drum—something that was not present in their youth. "We were originally taught that the drum is a channel for the prayers and spirit of the people, and we love having the opportunity to manifest this aspect of our being in a safe and educational atmosphere," says Talyn. The couple looks forward to the possibility of the group one day producing a CD. In the meantime, they are happy to continue meeting new people along the powwow trail.

Vincent Jones, a drummer with Four Rivers Drum, grew up in Virginia's tidewater area and has been active with the group for more than five years. An African American and Native American—his Blackfoot name is Tallbear—he has encountered people who have exhibited racism toward him, as well as people who have embraced his ethnic mixture. In reality, only once did an African American argue with him that he could not be Native American. More often, he is approached by people asking if he is Native American as they seek guidance with their own heritage. He describes how he deals with people's inquiries, saying, "If people ask me if I am Native American, 100 percent of the time I say yes. If they ask if I am African American, 100 percent of the time I say yes. I am all that my ancestors were."

Vincent feels blessed to be part of both of his cultures, and his dual lineage is a great source of pride for him. His connection to his Native heritage is so strong that he says, "I've walked a Native American life since I could walk, even when I did not realize what I was doing." He also feels pride and gratitude for being part of Four Rivers Drum. He loves the energies of the individuals in the group and feels his spirit connect with their spirits. He says, "I would like to see Four Rivers grow as an ambassador of Native American heritage and not only promote the culture but touch others in ways they cannot imagine."

A former submarine engineer who moved to Virginia Beach, Virginia, in 1983, Michael Manard has no proof that he comes from Native lineage. Yet in spite of his French Canadian and German heritage, he feels strongly drawn to the brotherhood and sisterhood of Four Rivers Drum. Like Jane Price, Michael was asked to join the group, as a drummer, in the summer of 2008. His European ethnicity has spared him from experiencing racism firsthand. He has, however, seen it in action at the restaurant where Jane worked. There, an intoxicated patron claimed that he didn't have to take directions from her and used a very derogatory racist term. Michael was furious and tersely explained to him that her ancestors arrived on this continent about twenty thousand years before his, so he and his friends were actually the new arrivals here.

All things considered, Michael is very honored to have been accepted into Four Rivers Drum without any sort of judgment from the other members. For him, the weekly get-togethers provide a strong sense of musical fellowship as well as the kind of bonding that comes from feeling part of an extended family.

A newcomer to Four Rivers Drum, Harold Caldwell grew up in Southern California. His ancestry is both Native American, from the Lower Muscogee and Gros Ventre Tribes, and African American, and he has embraced aspects of both. He not only drums for Four Rivers but also dances in the tidewater area at powwows that include the Chickahominy and Nottoway Tribes of Virginia.

Harold, with his predominantly African American features, contends that embracing one's heritage is much more than just appearance. He has run up against some prejudice concerning his Native heritage, but he tries to convey, "Native America has many colors." That is precisely what he loves about Four Rivers Drum—it honors this belief about Native America.

Singers with Four Rivers Drum for about two years, Shonda Buchanan and Afiya Owens Khalfani are mother and daughter. Shonda grew up in Kalamazoo, Michigan, although her parents trace their ancestors to North Carolina, which explains their Coharie, Neusiok, Eastern Band Cherokee, and Choctaw heritage. Shonda's Indian name is Rain and Afiya's is Little Star.

Shonda experiences racism frequently. When she asserts her Indian heritage, she has to tell people that she has traced her Native American lineage in order to erase their doubts. They seem to assume that her light skin comes from a mix of African and white ancestors. When she was growing up, she often heard the comment, "You've got that 'good' hair." She contends that the quality of her hair is the contribution of something many African Americans have but do not know they have—Native American ancestry.

Shonda and her daughter love the sense of camaraderie and friendship they find in Four Rivers Drum. "I love the community. I love the people," Shonda says simply.

Blake Artlip, a drummer with Four Rivers Drum for well over a year, was born in Muskegon, Michigan. His family has not lived on any of the eleven Indian reservations in Michigan since his full-blooded grandmother and the rest of her family were forced to leave their reservation when she was young. Because she was deaf, the Bureau of Indian affairs removed her so she could receive a "proper" education.

Blake has always been aware of his Ottawa tribal roots, but he went through life never feeling truly connected to his Native heritage. He has found that connection now in Four Rivers Drum. He says, "Right off the top, I connected with Michael and Bob." This is not surprising, considering the common heritage shared by Michael Cloud-Butler, Bob Jondreau, and Blake. The Ottawa, although politically independent from the Ojibwa and Chippewa, speak the same language, and all hail from the northern states of Michigan and Wisconsin. Blake says the three men are "from sister tribes, and I rely on them for much of my guidance regarding Native issues." In particular, he has learned about the sacredness of the drum and the importance of the tradition being passed on.

Because his family is far away in Michigan, he feels that the group has become like family. He finds comfort in the traditional Northern songs they sing and intends to continue singing and playing with them for many years to come.

Robert and Christine Narcomey have been with Four Rivers Drum for nearly four years, he as a drummer and she as a singer. Robert is Seminole and Navajo and was born and raised in Brigham City, Utah. Because his parents worked at the local school for the Native youth on the reservation, Robert was not allowed to attend it. In public school, he was ridiculed for not going to the Native school, while at home he endured comments about going to a "white" school.

After his school years, Robert set out to demonstrate for Native rights with the American Indian Movement, an activist organization. He traveled all over the country working as a carpenter and a welder, living at various times in Alabama, California, Louisiana, Texas, and Utah. He eventually made his way to Virginia as a shipbuilder. Following a similar path forged by his uncle, Will Sampson, the actor who played the shaman in *Poltergeist II*, Robert has appeared in the films *The New World* and *Pocahontas Revealed*.

In addition to also appearing in the films, Christine, Robert's wife, does Women's Traditional Dance, the oldest form of dance at powwows. Of Cherokee ancestry, Christine was born in Wilmington, North Carolina, in a time and place where Native people were told not to discuss and even to hide their Native heritage. Christine remembers a story from her mother's childhood that illustrates this apprehension about being openly Indian. When her mother was a child, she fell into a tub of boiling water and burned herself. Christine's grandfather went out to summon some people to help, and they put herbs on her. Upon hearing the story, Christine said to her mother, "Mom, those were medicine people." But Christine says her mother did not like to talk about it.

Four Rivers Drum

WHAT IS A POWWOW?

The term "powwow" originates from the Algonquian term *pau-wau*, which defined a gathering of medicine people or spiritual leaders. European explorers mispronounced the term as powwow and used it to describe almost any indigenous gathering. As the usage of English by indigenous people grew, "powwow" was the term accepted by Natives and non-Natives alike.

In the 1890s, traditional Indian dance was illegal under the Bureau of Indian Affairs (BIA). There is no recorded history of the first powwow held during this period, but evidence exists that in 1891 on the Flathead Indian Reservation in western Montana, tribal members attempted to hold a powwow on the Fourth of July. The BIA found it difficult to question celebrations on Independence Day, but Indian agency enforcers used the threat of the U.S. Army to disrupt and end the event.

Today, drum groups travel to powwows at the request of powwow organizers. The status of these groups varies, as does the respect that tribal members give to them. Members of drum groups consider the drum sacred and treat it with the utmost care and regard for its safekeeping. If a group playing the drum creates a song, that song belongs to it. There have been times when one group sang songs belonging to another group, and their drums were taken away from them.

Robert and Christine met at a Thanksgiving dinner in 2005. They began dating and were married the following year by a Monacan Indian spiritual leader. The couple joined Four Rivers Drum and love the sense of unity found in the group, calling it "a wonderful thing." "The singing group is like a family," says Robert. "I really enjoy the spiritual lift I get from being a part of it." Christine agrees, "The family is fantastic; when we get together, it is a great time." She describes the drum as healing, saying, "You may be down and out when you arrive, but when you listen, the drum just picks you back up."

Four Rivers Drum is similar to many of the drum groups that play at powwows large and small, offering its members a sense of culture, friendship, and belonging. Perhaps Sylvia Nery-Strickland says it best, "Our energy is good and, I believe, healing, so we can share and propagate." She says that many people have asked to attend their practice sessions, and those who did told her what a spiritual and uplifting experience they had. "They are almost changed people after the experience," she says. "I hope we can continue giving that to others."

With a wide variety of ethnicities and tribal affiliations among its members, Four Rivers Drum truly demonstrates love and acceptance of the wide array of colors present in Native America. Members of the group vary in appearance. Skin colors range from light to dark to varying shades in-between. But everyone is welcome. Everyone in the group is loved, respected, and honored equally. Four Rivers Drum lives and sings to the truest and highest spirit of the drum. The ancestors must be very proud.

Contact Four Rivers Drum
908 Adanka Lane
Virginia Beach, VA 23451
Website: www.fourriversdrum.com
Email: fourriversdrum@cox.net

Jamie Coon

VOCALIST COMBINING JAZZ AND POP ROCK

I t isn't easy to put a label on a musical style that sometimes sounds mellow and tender with a jazzy vibe, other times moves with an upbeat pop/rock energy, and still other times takes a cue from the greats of soul. This melding of styles describes the beautiful and creative music of one of the freshest new voices to come along in a while—the singer Jamie Coon.

Jamie's father is Creek and Seminole, two closely related tribes that originally inhabited the southeastern United States. Her mother is Creek and Irish. Jamie was raised in Oklahoma in the town of Okemah, which was named after Chief Okemah of the Kickapoo Tribe, and roughly translates as "things up high" in the Kickapoo language. Okemah is perhaps best known as the hometown of folk singer Woody Guthrie.

Jamie came from a big family of six brothers and sisters. Her parents played a huge part in influencing her musically. Her mother is an exceptional

Jamie Coon

singer who at one time performed in shows, and her father also sings and plays the mandolin. The household listened to a variety of musical genres and musicians, including legendary country artists such as Ronnie Milsap, early and later rock and rollers such as Fats Domino and Elton John, and classic soul artists such as Percy Sledge and Aretha Franklin. Jamie's favorite musician among the early legends, however, was the great Elvis Presley.

From the time she was very young, Jamie knew that she wanted to perform. Growing up in a household surrounded by so many siblings—"It was definitely not quiet," she remembers—gave her a readymade audience to listen to her sing. She began exploring music from several perspectives, trying out a few musical instruments. She took piano and guitar lessons and enjoyed playing these instruments, but practicing was odd to Jamie. She was being taught what she felt were childish songs on the piano when she was accustomed to listening to more complicated, advanced styles. Jamie remembers, "I was learning songs like 'Mary Had a Little Lamb,' but I wanted to play Elvis or Elton John. I wasn't too keen on the practicing thing."

Jamie was content living life as an ordinary kid. Although she knew that in order to be successful in life she would need to apply herself in school as well as focus on music, she says she approached her studies with an easy-going attitude: "I was fairly well liked in school, and I was pretty laid back. I was friends with everyone and school was great. I loved school and I had fun." She jokes that although she was a good student who never got into trouble or was given detention, she did have one small problem: "I was always running late!"

As a school kid, Jamie maintained a curiosity about her Native heritage. She and her family were not able to attend powwows, which would have put her directly in touch with her Native culture, so she actively sought information. For three years, she attended a summer school program for Native kids only. She sincerely loved the program, which not only provided information about Native heritage and history but also offered hands-on crafts activities such as basketmaking.

In fifth grade, Jamie began playing in her school band and continued to play into high school. She started out on the drums, for which she showed a real talent, but she was really drawn to vocal music. She knew she wanted to sing and began taking vocal lessons.

As she made her way through elementary school and into high school, Jamie knew that in spite of her young age, she was in charge of her life. In order to be successful, she would have to commit herself to achieving greatness by making positive choices one by one, even if others around her were making negative choices. As she describes it, "In high school, I knew people who did a lot of drinking. I was usually the designated driver. I knew what I wanted to do at a very young age. I knew what I had to do to get there. My mind was focused on what I could do for my music."

She formed a band with some high school friends. Still wanting to experiment with different aspects of music, she played bass and did some singing. The band played at multiple venues, including a local college and some local talent shows. In fact, Jamie decided that every chance she got, she would sign up for talent shows. Did she win every single competition she entered? Absolutely not. She says, "I think I won one or two, but I got beaten a lot. It was disappointing. Your family believes in you; they always think you are the best."

Jamie was learning that winning and losing were just part of the territory of a musician, and that no one could win all the time: "I would pout for about three or four minutes, but I would use that energy to push me forward and go further

Jamie Coon and her grandparents

instead of being upset about it." By competing, win or lose, she was practicing how to grow and perform as an artist and how to put herself out there in front of people. She began to see that singing as a career was a definite possibility.

After graduating from high school, Jamie got a full-time job in Okemah. Her heart was still in music, though, and she dreamed of being a singer. She decided to reach for the stars and take action. She put together a demo tape and applied to the Musicians Institute in Hollywood, California, as a vocalist major. To Jamie's excitement and surprise, she was accepted.

But Jamie's family was shocked when she told them about her acceptance to the Musicians Institute. She would be the first of the family to leave home. Her mother was particularly emotional, begging her not to go to California. Jamie says, "I knew it wasn't because she didn't believe in me; she just didn't want me to leave." Her dad stood behind her and managed to calm down her mother.

Jamie was overwhelmed with excitement and happiness as she prepared for her trip to California. While she packed her belongings, her mind raced with countless thoughts. She had never lived anywhere other than Oklahoma and had never even been to California. She remembers thinking, on the way to the airport, "Oh, my gosh, I am really leaving my family and leaving everything I know, and I'm going to a place where no one I know lives. I will be living by myself." Her nervousness really hit her a few hours before the plane left. Fortunately, her father had decided to go to California with her to help her get started in a new place.

Jamie discovered soon enough that Hollywood wasn't all glamour. She came into contact with sights and situations, some of them scary, that weren't exactly listed in the travel brochures. Homelessness, for example, was something she had never seen in her small town in Oklahoma.

Jamie had to get settled into her new life in the big city before school started. She describes what it was like for her in the beginning, when she and her dad were out looking for an

Jamie Coon and her sisters

apartment: "We went to this little restaurant on Hollywood Boulevard that is no longer there. I am not a person who shows a lot of emotion, but I started crying because I didn't want my father to leave me." He decided to stay an additional three days to provide support and be there for her. When he flew home, Jamie was left to fend for herself. She was living in a new place, Hollywood, and she didn't know anyone there.

Once school started and she was able to throw herself completely into her classes, Jamie didn't have much time to fear her situation. The Musicians Institute turned out to be a true source of inspiration and joy for Jamie. At first, as someone from a small town trying to fulfill her dreams in the big city, she was shy. But the school gave her the confidence to pursue her goal of becoming a professional singer. Jamie says, "It was absolutely great! I had so much support from that school and the teachers. One thing it gave me was a belief in myself." In her studies, she pursued excellence. In time, she earned due recognition for her hard work and received the Outstanding Student of the Year award.

After finishing school, Jamie buckled down to pursue her true goal in life. She formed a group and began trying to obtain gigs at local establishments. She credits her unshakeable belief in herself for getting her through these uncertain times: "When you are going after something you have wanted for a long time, it's scary. Getting gigs is scary. But you just keep on trucking. When other people around you see you believing in yourself, you attract people who believe in you too. A belief in yourself is truly the key."

In the midst of pursuing her career, Jamie got a job in the music field at an audio company in Los Angeles. This put her in the promising position of working in an environment where she was constantly in contact with people who were connected to the music industry and who could appreciate her music and possibly help her career. She wasn't afraid to take matters into her own hands. For example, when she met a recent graduate from a Seattle music-recording school who was just kicking off a career in Los Angeles as a producer, she gave him a demo tape of one of her songs, "Waiting." When he expressed enthusiasm for the song, Jamie knew she was on the right track.

Emboldened, she put together a benefit show at the Hollywood Improv. It was at this event that Jamie's career in music would take a substantial turn in a positive direction. The benefit, which featured comedians and musicians, was attended by representatives from RipTide Music, based in Santa Monica, California. RipTide is a music licensing and publishing company that places music in television, movie trailers, film, and other outlets. Jamie's band and singing impressed the folks from RipTide, and one of them handed her his business card. Soon afterward, she and the band received a publishing deal with RipTide. One year after signing with the company, Jamie was overwhelmed when her song "Waiting" was featured on an episode of the TV show *The Ghost Whisperer*.

"Waiting" has been described by reviewers as "catchy," "cool," and "a gem of a song." But Jamie wasn't satisfied with having just one song to her name. She worked hard, along with her band members, to create their first CD, *Everything So Far*, on the independent label CSW Entertainment, in 2005. Within a relatively short time, she and the band began receiv-

ing quite a bit of notice and considerable critical acclaim for the
album—especially noteworthy
for a first independently produced album and a singer fairly
new to the music scene. Two
of its songs appeared on the
soundtrack of the comedy film
Long-Term Relationship, and the
single "Breathe" is featured in
the film *Deceit.*

Jamie Coon

The list of nominations and
awards generated by *Everything
So Far* is impressive and long.
Jamie was nominated for Best
Female Artist at the First Annual Southern California Music
Awards in 2006. In 2007, she was nominated for Best New
Artist and Best Pop Recording at the prestigious Native Ameri-
can Music Awards. That same year, she won Best Out of County
at the Orange County Music Awards. The Payne County Line/
Oklahoma Music Awards voted her Singer/Songwriter of the
Year in 2007, Female Vocalist of the Year in 2008, and nomi-
nated her song "Waiting" for Single of the Year that same year.
Both "Waiting" and "Breathe" won Mainstream Song of the Year
at the First Annual Native-E Music Awards, where Jamie was
also nominated as Songwriter of the Year for "Waiting."

Jamie continues to perform and promote her music as
she and her band members work on new projects. She performed to sold-out audiences at the Smithsonian's National
Museum of the American Indian Summer Music Festival
and the Kennedy Center, both in Washington, DC. She also
entertained on the stage of the thousand-seat Palace of Fine
Arts Theatre in San Francisco at the American Indian Film
Festival award show.

Her goal is to be on tour three to six months out of the
year. Although she is now far removed from the small town

where she grew up, Jamie has not forgotten and never will forget where she came from: "I was that little sixth grader who always wanted to be a musician." She offers advice to young people interested in seeking a career as an artist: "First of all, love yourself and believe in yourself. Be proud of who you are and be true to yourself, and I guarantee that everything you want in life will happen. You are going to get negativity; that's always going to happen, but you can't let that get you down."

Jamie certainly has experienced her share of racial tension and felt her share of criticism. She sometimes feels that she gets passed by because she's not, in her words, "your typical Britney Spears or Christina Aguilera type." But Jamie is proud of her heritage and lists herself as a Native American singer and songwriter. She still runs into some degree of ignorance today, reflected in the odd questions and comments she occasionally gets, such as: "Oh, you're an Indian? Did you grow up in a tipi?" and "You must be rich with all those casinos!" Jamie says she just looks at folks who make such comments and smiles.

As she strives to maintain her growing status as a working artist, Jamie knows that there will always be obstacles. But she believes that obstacles make her better, and she doesn't let them stop her from striving to succeed. In fact, she says, "Whenever anyone told me it wasn't possible, I did it." Experiencing any kind of difficulty won't stand in the way of the talented Jamie Coon, not with her attitude: "I don't really think about it. It's just something to overcome while I keep working on my music."

In keeping with her practice of advising young people, Jamie offers to communicate directly: "If any young people have questions, they can email me at jamiecoon@jamie coon.com."

Contact Jamie Coon
Website: www.jamiecoon.com
To contact Jamie, sign up on the website.

Mato Nanji

GUITARIST AND LEADER OF
THE BAND INDIGENOUS

I f blues-rock is the music that speaks to you, then look no further than guitarist Mato Nanji, leader of the band Indigenous. Since the band's beginning in 1998, his soulful voice and wailing guitar have been turning out some of the best, genuinely serious blues-rock sounds wherever the band plays across the United States.

Mato Nanji, whose name means "Standing Bear" in the Nakota language, grew up on the Yankton Sioux Indian Reservation in South Dakota as a member of the Nakota

Mato Nanji and Indigenous

Sioux Tribe. Mato was part of a very large family. His father, Greg Zephier, had several children before he met Mato's mother, who came into the relationship with two children of her own. They then had four children together. In total, there are fourteen children.

As a child, Mato lived with financial hardship. All around him on the reservation, located in the middle of farmland, he saw despair and addiction. In spite of these difficulties, Mato did not think he had it worse than anybody else and maintained a positive attitude. He concedes that "it's rough growing up on the reservation" but considers it like any other town, with bad areas and good areas. He says, "In the bad part of any town, you are going to see the same drugs and alcohol or whatever. I have traveled around the country and in every city I see, it is pretty much the same."

Fortunately for Mato, he was introduced to music at an early age, and it gave him something positive to focus on to avoid the negativity around him. His father, Greg, also became involved with music early, taking up the drums when he was only eight years old. In the 1960s and 1970s, Greg had a band that played traditional rock and roll. In fact, it was his father's record collection—which included albums by such great blues and rock musicians as Buddy Guy, Jimi Hendrix, B. B. King, Santana, and Led Zeppelin— that inspired Mato. Listening to these musicians at home while he was growing up made Mato want to emulate them.

In middle school, Mato watched his brother play a trumpet solo in a school band performance. Impressed, Mato chose to play the trombone in the sixth-grade band. Wanting to follow in his brother's footsteps, he begged the bandleader for a solo piece to play. The bandleader gave him his opportunity during a practice session, handing Mato the sheet music to a Beethoven piece. But he refused to look at the sheet music, instead letting loose on his instrument in an amazing display of talent. According to Mato, the bandleader then asked him to keep to the sheet music in consideration of the other band members, none of whom showed the same advanced musical ability.

As a young kid, Mato also banged on "pots and pans and ice-cream buckets," wanting to play the drums as his father had as a child. But, remembers Mato, "with the drums, I never could get anything really going." Greg, his father, had evolved into a guitar player, and eventually Mato followed suit. Playing his father's albums as guides, he picked up the guitar and tentatively began to re-create the sounds he was hearing. When his dad saw his interest, he taught Mato how to tune the instrument. However, Greg would not actually teach him how to play. Instead, Mato remembers, he would say, "Sit down and listen to this record and learn it yourself. That is the way I learned. When you learn that way, you never forget it." Mato's dad coached him through by listening to him and catching things. Talented as Mato is, he says that his dad "could hear a song or hear a lick and he would just know it instantly and know what the chord was. I still cannot do it today. He was that kind of musician."

Childhood was full of challenges for Mato. He did the best he could to continue practicing at home while facing the realities of life on his reservation. The school, unfortunately, did not provide enough of a creative outlet for him, and he struggled. Adding to his frustration was the prevalence of racism on the reservation. Mato says it still exists and is, in fact, as bad as ever. But growing up with his father taught him to "take the good with the bad." His dad did not let racism affect him, because, Mato says, "He was more of a civil-rights kind of person. If anybody needed help, regardless of his race, he would be there."

The difficulties he encountered every day compelled Mato to study music even harder. Around eighth grade and entering high school, he completely embraced the guitar, playing well enough by this time to perform as a solo musician. He started performing a little earlier than everybody else, playing with a couple of other bands composed of local guys: "We played at high schools and stuff like that. It was pretty fun."

Eventually Mato joined efforts with his brother Pte (Peh-tay), who played bass, and his sister Wanbdi (Wan-ba-dee), who played drums. With the encouragement of Mato's parents to become a band, they named themselves Indigenous. They practiced for about two or three years, learning "a bunch of songs." From the start, Mato's dad told him to learn from different musicians and groups, take from each one what he could, and then write his own music.

When Mato was around seventeen, he and his siblings, with the help of their father, began getting gigs at local venues with small audiences. Their very first gigs were mostly in front of family and friends. Although the band sang cover songs of artists such as Santana and Jimi Hendrix, they also had a few songs of their own. One of the first songs Mato remembers writing was called "Things We Do."

By this time, Mato had decided to pursue music above everything else and made every effort to build a career on the stage. He recalls, "I concentrated on music 100 percent, and

Indigenous

we just hit the road." The band found a booking agent from Nebraska and began touring heavily. His parents had to accompany Mato because he was too young, at seventeen, to play in some of the clubs without them. Initially, Indigenous was composed of Mato and his brother and sister. Their cousin, Horse, joined the group as a percussionist a little later. Mato explains, "He was having trouble in school and having a hard time. We asked him to come play with us, and it gave him an outlet. He ended up fitting in with the band really well."

Mato and Indigenous continued to tour. He was at last doing what he loved, but being on the road was rough, and the family band experienced a couple of unfortunate setbacks. A house fire destroyed several of the band's instruments, and they lost some equipment in a burglary. Nevertheless, Indigenous persevered.

As their touring continued, the group's reputation grew. In September 1998, Indigenous landed a record deal. The manager they had at the time found a label, Pachyderm Records, which was just getting started. Although Mato had been immersed in music for a while, the album was like a fresh beginning, like the band was just getting started. He describes the feeling: "Just going into the studio, it felt really good, because my dad was still alive, and he was there when we were recording that record. He was a big part of it. He always encouraged me to write original music, so that record ended up being all original music. *Things We Do* was the first album we put out nationwide."

With the release of *Things We Do*, Indigenous found success and recognition. In 1999, the album was played on radio stations all across the country, and their first single on the album, "Now That You're Gone," became the fifteenth most played rock and roll song in the United States, according to the *Lakota Times*. Even more groundbreaking, the single reached number twenty-two on Billboard's Mainstream Rock chart, making Indigenous one of the first Native American bands to achieve that height in mainstream rock music.

Along with the popularity generated by the public's embrace of *Things We Do* came recognition from the Native American music industry, as the nominations and awards started to roll in. After the video for the lead single and title track, "Things We Do," was released, it went on to receive first place at the American Indian Film Festival, was shown three times at the Sundance Film Festival, and was nominated for Best Music Video at the Second Annual (1999) Native American Music Awards. Mato and Indigenous went on to win three Nammys that same year: Album of the Year, Group of the Year, and Best Pop Group.

On a creative streak, Indigenous released an EP, *Blues This Morning*, and a full-length album, *Live at Pachyderm Studio 1998*. The band ended up winning two Nammys at the Third Annual (2000) Native American Music Awards, for Best Blues Recording and Group of the Year. But Indigenous was not done yet; they got right back to the studio at Pachyderm Records and released *Circle*. This bluesy album gained considerable acclaim and popularity, and with it the band broke new ground again, climbing to the number three spot on Billboard's Top Blues Albums chart.

After the release of *Circle*, Mato decided he wanted to modify the style of music the band was putting out. The group worked together to create a heavier sound. In addition, they signed with a larger record label, Silvertone Records. In 2003, the band's self-titled album, *Indigenous*, was released and soon duplicated *Circle*'s success by gaining the number three spot on Billboard's Top Blues Albums chart. Mato remembers *Indigenous*, featuring "Come on Suzy" and "What You Do to Me," as their first major-label release: "We were trying to move into a heavier theme at that time. All of the other albums were a little mellower. But I think with each record, we did something a little different, which I like to do. I like to explore different things."

In 2005, Indigenous left Silvertone Records and produced another EP, titled *Long Way Home*, on their own record label, Indigenous Records. A year later, the group signed with Vanguard Records. Around this time period, Mato began feeling some tension among the members of the band. However, the group forged ahead and released *Chasing the Sun* in 2006. This album became their most successful of all, reaching the number two spot on Billboard's Top Blues Albums chart.

Although the members of Indigenous, with their last album, had yet again achieved creative and commercial success, they agreed that it was time for them to move in different directions. They had been talking about it for a while. Wanbdi, Mato's sister, was burnt out from the constant touring and did not want to be on the road anymore. Pte, his brother, wanted to start his own group and do his own music, with which Mato had no problem.

In fact, Mato welcomed the change of pace. He wanted to reclaim Indigenous as his own and pursue his own personal musical path. Keeping the name Indigenous alive was important to him because he felt it connected so well with the music. He says, "Music is universal, and the name Indigenous is universal as well, because we are all indigenous." He explains his feelings about the split: "I just decided to keep the name going and keep the music going. It is not really that much of a change, other than I am still learning and I am still moving forward. It was tough, moving away from my brother and sister. But you just have to do what you have to do." A major change that made the transition even greater was that Mato had met and married a woman named Leah. In addition to their relationship as husband and wife, they were also partners in music.

By 2008, Mato had formed the new Indigenous, consisting of guitarist Kris Lager, keyboardist Jeremiah Weir, bassist Aaron C. Wright, and drummers John Fairchild and Kirk Stallings. Together, the group worked diligently to create the album *Broken Lands*, recorded at Winterland Studios in Minneapolis, Minnesota. Leah Nanji, Mato's wife,

Mato Nanji and Indigenous

sang backup vocals, and Chico Perez played percussion. *Broken Lands* was released through Vanguard Records on August 19, 2008. It was the first album with no original Indigenous members on it other than Mato.

Mato felt good about the new album. He acknowledges that working together as a group, always having to come together to talk about new material, can be tough for any band. But he says that he finally got to make the album the way he wanted to, a more personal album. For example, the title of the album, *Broken Lands*, was up for discussion. It comes from a lyric ("all is lost in these broken lands") in one of the album's songs, "Place I Know." The group also considered the song's title for the album's title. But Mato says they settled on *Broken Lands* because this phrase "stems back to where I grew up on my reservation. That is kind of what the song is about, growing up in rough neighborhoods and tough times."

The musical styles of *Broken Lands* have his signature all over them, too. Mato says, "I really wanted to make this record like the old records I grew up listening to." To make the album capture more of a live feel, which Mato had always wanted to get as close to as possible, he separated two of the guitar parts into different speakers, "kind of like Hendrix used to do." Satisfied with the results, he says, "We came pretty close."

On the song "I Can't Pretend," which Mato calls "probably my favorite song on the album," he went for something a little different from his previous albums, describing the song as having "that Eagles kind of country-rock feel to it." The song "Let it Rain," on the other hand, has a simple intro, which he added at the studio, that he describes as "kind of like a Stones or Black Crowes kind of thing."

After touring all over the United States for *Broken Lands*, Mato took part in the Experience Hendrix Tour 2008, a four-week concert tour and tribute to the influential, ground-

"Eyes of a Child" from *Broken Lands*

There is nowhere you can't go
You've taught me what I need to know
Living with no envy, loving all around
Finding your voice with each new sound

Chorus:
Don't you wish that you could see
Through the eyes of a child
Such a beautiful thing to me
Through the eyes of a child

Gaining strength from the arms that embrace you
Never worry of the troubles that may face you
Teaching others life is a gift
With every smile you will get your wish

breaking guitarist Jimi Hendrix. Mato, along with an amazing array of other super-talented musicians, played Hendrix classics to huge audiences across the country from coast to coast. The lineup was long and included legendary blues guitarist Buddy Guy; Billy Cox, bass guitarist for Hendrix; contemporary guitarists Jonny Lang, Kenny Wayne Shepherd, and Eric Johnson; Cesar Rojas and David Hidalgo of Los Lobos; Aerosmith's Brad Whitford; and Chris Layton, drummer for the late Stevie Ray Vaughan.

Mato's advice to kids who are thinking about pursuing music as a profession is straightforward: "I think if it is something that you really, really want to do, then do it." But he tempers that statement with a reminder that the music business is very difficult, and he cannot honestly say that striving for a career in music is the right thing for everyone to do. He advises young folks to stay in school and do what they can to learn as much as they can, even if it is learning about the music business. "That," he says, "is the right thing to do." He pulls no punches, admitting that "the business is really all about money." Although he says that this fact "stinks," he recognizes that in order to survive, you have to make money.

Mato Nanji

"But that is not what it is about for me. It never has been, but you have to eat," he says simply, expressing so well the age-old conflict between following your heart and making a living.

Talent aside, Mato has been lucky. The music business is "rough," in his words, but he's on the road doing what he wants to do. However, success wasn't just handed to him. Growing up, he threw himself into music. When he woke up in the morning, he grabbed his guitar and practiced. He practiced constantly, keeping at it. "That is all I did. I did not do anything else," he recalls. Even to this day, he still picks up his guitar, which sits right next to his bed, and plays a little acoustic. He explains, "I grab it and get an idea. It has to be in you. It is not something that you can explain to anybody. It is just there; I do not know what it is."

With multiple Native American Music Awards and several high-ranking albums on the Billboard charts, Mato and Indigenous have been a formidable force on the rock and blues music scenes. Now, with his new band members, his sights are set even higher: "We are still working on breaking out and going international. I still am excited about doing that. We have been doing a lot more concert dates, and slowly we are getting to where we want to be worldwide."

If history is any indication of success, then Mato and Indigenous, with their talent, determination, and know-how, will achieve his dream of going international. From the very beginning of Indigenous, when the band was first formed, Mato has stayed true to the words of his father, "Always do your own music." The crowds that come to listen and the fans who buy his music surely sense that Mato Nanji has done just that and just as surely will help propel Indigenous into a worldwide market.

Contact Mato Nanji and Indigenous

Website: www.indigenousmusic.net

To contact Mato or the band members, click the "contact" button on the website.

Shane Yellowbird

COUNTRY MUSIC SINGER

If you are under the impression that all country music artists are from the South, or even the United States, think again. Shane Yellowbird, rising country music star, is from Hobbema, in Alberta, Canada.

Within five years of signing with the music label 306 Records, Shane was climbing the charts with top-ten hits on Canadian radio and turning on fans with his music videos on television. Interestingly, he began his musical aspirations as a competitor in karaoke contests. His voice so impressed audiences, judges, and, ultimately, industry professionals that he was able to make the transition to country music professional.

To some people, standing in front of an audience and singing a karaoke song may not seem like a huge accomplishment. But for Shane it was a significant achievement. From a very young age, he has had a serious stuttering problem, a condition that made him extremely self-conscious. But

Shane Yellowbird

Shane decided to push himself in spite of this obstacle and go for success in a very risky business. It was not easy, but his investment has paid off a hundredfold, and he is now one of Canada's hottest country music stars.

Shane is Cree, the largest First Nations group in Canada, with over 200,000 registered members and dozens of self-governed nations. He grew up on the Hobbema Reservation in Alberta under the strict rule of his father, Murray Albert Yellowbird. Murray was strict because of his own upbringing. The oldest boy of nine children in a family whose father worked away from home a lot of the time, Murray took on the role of parental figure, dropping out of school in the tenth grade to work on the farm to support his younger siblings.

Murray met and married Colleen Buffalo when they were both still teenagers. They had two children three years apart, Carmen and Shane. When Shane was still very young, his parents broke up; in fact, Shane doesn't even remember them being together. His father eventually remarried, had more children, and raised them as a strict disciplinarian.

In retrospect, Shane realizes that having a strict father kept him on the right track and away from negative influences. He describes what it was like growing up in his circumstances: "Hobbema can be a negative place. Not too many people in Hobbema at that time finished school. My cousins were into drugs, gangs, and stuff like that. But my tough dad kept me away from those things. I stayed busy with friends who were into sports. I had hockey linemates who were closer than cousins of mine were. I spent a lot of my time staying over at friends' houses. If I was not playing hockey, I was playing basketball or track. I just kept busy."

Although Shane was involved with sports and other activities, he had a difficult time socially. His severe stutter caused him great anguish and insecurity beyond typical adolescent shyness. Normal activities involving oral communication posed a tough challenge, and he was actually afraid to talk.

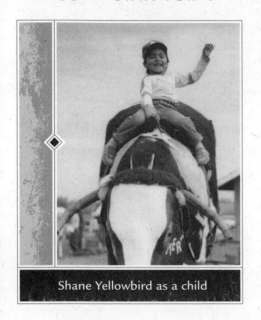

Shane Yellowbird as a child

Shane's condition was not his fault. Stuttering is approximately 60 percent hereditary, and Shane's grandfather and aunt on his mother's side stuttered. His family knew to address his problem and sent Shane to a speech therapist when he was nine. He was so self-conscious and hesitant to speak that he did not want to talk to the therapist. In time, however, the therapist taught Shane different methods to cope with his speaking problems. One solution in particular may have paved the way for Shane's career as a country music artist.

Shane recalls, "When I was a kid, my therapist suggested singing the words, and I thought it was the stupidest thing ever." But Shane was willing to give it a try around people he trusted. He began to tap on his leg to give himself a beat and then sing whatever he wanted to communicate, such as asking his dad if he could spend the night at a friend's house. He discovered that singing to a rhythmic beat allowed him to speak more fluidly, and he still uses this trick, especially in a situation that makes him nervous, such as a television interview.

Although singing words controlled his stutter to an extent, Shane still held back in many social situations. He was the target of a lot of ridicule and constant jokes. Most of the time, he would simply not speak. He recalls, "It was very frustrating. I was a small kid. I was tall, but I was skinny. I was bullied a lot and teased. It was tough." Even on the ice during a hockey game, his stutter would emerge under stress, and his opponents would ridicule him for his speech problem.

As Shane began approaching his teen years, he found it more difficult to manage his expanding social life without speaking. He knew he was going to have to address his speech problem eventually: "I was becoming involved with meeting people in school and sports, and it was hard for me to speak to them. I was somewhat quiet; I did not really let people know about my speech problem until I got close to them." Tired of being the subject of ridicule for such a long time, he decided to make a change. He says, "One day I remember getting up and saying, 'You've got to get over this, man!'" He was not going to let his situation defeat him.

With that decision, Shane empowered himself to do better. He began to watch for words that would initiate his stutter. Certain words—trigger words—cause him to regress to the way he spoke when he was young. It has taken him twenty-eight years to avoid and master these trigger words. "That means," he explains, "if I do a radio interview, I have to think very quickly how I am going to answer and not use those words. One of those words is my name. I have a hard time with *s* words, anything that starts with *s*."

Ironically, although Shane's speech improved when he entered high school, he found that something else made it hard for him to fit in socially—something that defines his very essence. Shane explains, "One of the biggest problems I had when I was growing up was that I hung out with a lot of non-Native people. All of my best friends were white people. If I was hanging around with my white friends, I was known as the Native guy. If I was hanging out with the Native people, they would always call me the white boy because I had an education and dressed differently or had a job and was making money. It

Shane Yellowbird as a child

was very tough when I was in my teens; I did not know where I belonged."

After high school, Shane applied to Red Deer College in Alberta, where he majored in Fine Arts because of his love for drawing and painting. All his life he had used drawing as his getaway. But once in college, he struggled with some of the required subjects, particularly art history. For an hour and a half, three times a week, he sat in a dark auditorium looking at slides. The instructor would explain who did the drawing or painting, what year it was done, its title, what medium was used, and why the artist did the piece. Shane says, "I took the class three times and I could not pass it."

Shane did the best he could in college, but finally decided it was not for him. At age twenty-one, with growing confidence in his ability to speak more fluidly, he decided to start taking risks doing something he loved to do—sing. Shane entered a karaoke contest in the town of Ponoka, near Hobbema. The host of the contest, noticing Shane's potential, told him about other contests. Soon he was not only overcoming his speech problems and his shyness with people, but he was also winning the contests he entered.

Shane auditioned as an entertainer, along with hundreds of others, for the 2001 Truck Stampede competition. He was chosen as one of the top ten who would compete onstage at a grandstand show. This was his first time on such a large stage, in front of an audience of a thousand that included his parents and cousins. Shane remembers, "I did two songs, and I did not want to get off that stage." When, to his excitement, he won the competition, he began to compete with new confidence, entering and winning such competitions as the Canadian Finals Rodeo and the Big Valley Jamboree.

One cold winter night, Shane's stepfather met by chance a country music manager, who invited Shane into his office. They talked over coffee, and the manager subsequently booked Shane into a couple of shows. Because the manager was leaving the business, he had Shane meet with Louis O'Reilly of

O'Reilly International Entertainment Management and 306 Records, based in Saskatoon, Saskatchewan, Canada. O'Reilly was concerned both about Shane's stutter and the fact that he had gotten somewhat of a late start in his career. But after speaking with Shane and realizing the serious obstacles he had overcome in his life, O'Reilly became convinced that the singer possessed the determination to succeed in the music industry.

O'Reilly put Shane to work performing at numerous venues, "paying his dues," as O'Reilly puts it. They both wanted to make sure that Shane got it right. Finally, after two years of auditioning a multitude of potential band members and going through a thousand songs in order to come up with the perfect ten, Shane and 306 Records produced an album. *Life Is Calling My Name* was released in November 2006. Critics raved, and Shane found himself skyrocketing into the Canadian spotlight.

Shane could hardly believe that he was becoming a well-known country singer. His excitement increased when he learned that he would be filming his first music video. The actual making of it, however, was an eye-opener for him. His impression of country music videos on television was that they looked like a lot of fun. The reality was that a three-and-a-half-minute video was the result of a twenty-hour day of hard work consisting of a lot of "hurry-up and waits" and makeup redoing. Shane quickly lost his unrealistic illusions about making videos.

Life Is Calling My Name achieved incredible success, and the recognition and awards started rolling in. Shane won three awards at the 2006 Aboriginal People's Choice Music Awards: Best New Artist, Single of the Year, and Best Music Video for "Beautiful Concept." Four of the CD's singles eventually became top-ten hits on the Canadian Country Singles chart. His third single, "Pickup Truck," was one of the ten most played country songs in 2007 in Canada, becoming his first top-five song on the Canadian Country Singles Chart. At the 2007 Canadian Country Music

Awards, Shane was the Chevy Trucks Rising Star of the Year Award winner, an achievement that came with the great bonus of a brand-new truck.

Shane opened the 2007 Aboriginal Peoples Choice Music Awards, where he won Aboriginal Entertainer of the Year, Best Country CD for *Life Is Calling My Name*, and Best Music Video for "Pickup Truck." He was also nominated for the 2008 Juno Award—Canada's music awards—for Country Recording of the Year. In November of that same year, Shane's song "I Remember the Music," from *Life Is Calling My Name*, received the award for Best Music Video at the Aboriginal Peoples Choice Music Awards.

In six years, Shane had made the transition from a shy person shackled by a stutter to a Canadian country music star. Still amazed, Shane says, "If you had come up to me in 2001 and told me that in a half dozen years I would be one of the top Canadian country artists, I would have laughed and said you were out of your mind. Five years later, I've had nineteen nominations and number-one hits on the radio, and I received a Country Rising Star of the Year Award in Canada."

His success may propel him into the United States as well, elevating his status to international country music celebrity. To Shane, it is barely believable, unaccustomed as he is to the attention he is now getting. Everywhere he goes, whether he's at a Calgary Flames game, going to the pool, or out for a bite to eat, people ask him for his autograph. Although he sometimes feels he does not have as much privacy as he would like, he takes it all in stride. As Shane explains, nothing compares to the excitement he feels when singing to his fans. That is the best part for him. He says, "You could have had a horrible show, or lighting problems, but then you sign autographs afterward, and you meet the people and they say, 'We love you.' Even if you do a bad show, you know that you helped people have a good time."

Shane also talks openly about what it feels like to be an Aboriginal musician and representative of his culture: "I love that I inspire the Native kids on my reservation. I'm proud of who I am and always have been." When he performs at a gig on a reservation and is asked to talk to the kids, he gets nervous because of his stutter. But he thinks it's probably helpful for them to see him as he really is, or as he puts it, to see him "falter a little bit." He doesn't often bring up Native topics, having found that people sometimes judge him because he left the reservation and its school to further his education and career.

His fans know that Shane is a great singer and someone who connects strongly with his heritage. What they don't know about him is that he is a huge practical joker, especially with his bandmates. Occasionally, Shane is the butt of the joke, like the time his bass player put toothpaste on a phone and Shane got it on his ear. But Shane knows how to take his revenge to the next level. While on stage singing a slow ballad together, he and his bass player were one-upping each other on high notes. Just as Shane was about to hit a really high note, he pulled away from the microphone, leaving his bandmate screaming alone into the mic in a high-pitched voice. Shane says he was laughing so hard, he just about fell off his stool. He recalls, "My guitar player was laughing, the whole crowd was laughing, and he was just looking at me, shaking his head."

Shane Yellowbird

Shane played another practical joke when the band was on a plane. The flight attendant noticed him and asked for his autograph. The bass player, who gets motion sickness and was nauseated at the time, had gotten Shane with a joke earlier. So Shane told the flight attendant that it was the bass player's birthday, and she announced it on the intercom. Unfortunately, the bass player was throwing up at the time into the airsickness bag. He just managed to stand up and wave to everybody.

Practical jokes aside, Shane and his career show no signs of slowing down. In September 2008, he performed at the American Institute for Stuttering Gala in New York City. The event raised $350,000 to be used for children needing speech therapy. But in Shane's opinion, his biggest career victory so far was receiving the Rising Star Award, because he was up against such stiff competition. It was a victory he shared with his parents, who couldn't make it to the award show, and all of Hobbema.

Shane still tries to find time to paint and draw whenever he has a free moment. But with his career in high gear, these moments are few. Living his dream as a country star, he advises people who have their own dreams to succeed in the music business to never give up: "This business is so up and down. I have probably thought about quitting more times than I have thought about being nominated for an award or having a hit. But you've got to keep going."

Shane Yellowbird is one to know. Not only has he succeeded in an industry that is difficult for anyone trying his luck, but he has done it with an additional obstacle. He did not let his stutter stand in his way. He has become what he is today with some luck, a lot of hard work and determination, and a whole lot of singing and songwriting talent. That talent will most assuredly continue to please his fans and the country music industry for years to come.

Contact Shane Yellowbird
Website: www.shaneyellowbird.com
To contact Shane, sign up on the website.

Gabriel Ayala

CLASSICAL GUITARIST

S ome music is so great that it has the capacity to transport us to another place or time, another realm. Some musicians are so good that we forget we are even listening to them play; we are only aware of the emotions their music creates in us. The music is fast and intense—we are happy and energized. Now it's slow and moody—we feel sad and pensive. Classical guitar is that kind of music, and Gabriel Ayala, classical guitarist, is that kind of musician.

Gabriel Ayala has played at such venues as the Gathering of Nations in Albuquerque, New Mexico, from 2005 to 2008, for over thirty thousand people; the John F. Kennedy Center for the Arts, in New York; and the National Museum for the American Indian, in Washington, DC. He has performed on live radio broadcasts and national and public television. Such success did not come without tremendous commitment and hard work.

Gabriel was born in 1972 in Corpus Christi, Texas, the largest city on the Texas coast

Gabriel Ayala

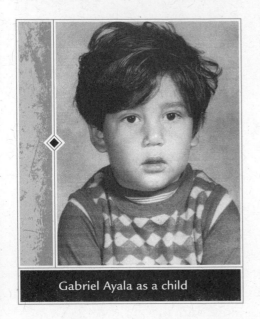

Gabriel Ayala as a child

and the sixth largest port in the nation. Although his family was not financially well off, they were definitely rich in one thing—relatives. As Gabriel describes it, "On my maternal side, I had sixteen aunts and uncles and over sixty cousins. The Creator really blessed me with tons of family."

Gabriel is Pascua Yaqui, a Native American tribe whose people originally resided in the desert areas of what is now Mexico, near Arizona. Spanish military repeatedly attacked the tribe, eventually forcing many to flee to Arizona territories. Today their main reservation is located in Tucson, Arizona, but for generations the tribe roamed extensively back and forth between Mexican and U.S. territories. When the borders between the two countries were established, many Pascua Yaqui were separated from their fellow tribal members. Of those who remained in Mexico, some, according to Gabriel, "were sold as slaves and taken all across Mexico," including many of his relatives.

Gabriel's grandfather, according to Gabriel's uncle, came up from Mexico to live in Texas after he had ridden with the Mexican revolutionary general Pancho Villa. Many Yaqui people moved to Arizona to escape the violence of the Mexican Revolution. It wasn't until 1939 that the Yaqui in Mexico were granted official recognition and title to their lands. The Yaqui in the United States, who were still considered Mexican, waited even longer. Thanks to the efforts of Anselmo Valencia Tori, former chairman of the Pascua Yaqui Association and former vice chairman of the Tribal Council, the Pascua Yaqui reservation in Arizona finally received federal recognition as sovereign in the United States on September 18, 1978.

Gabriel was grateful to hear his relatives tell the stories of his familial elders and felt fortunate that his grandmother primarily raised him. Although he grew up in a minority neighborhood, as a Yaqui child he sometimes felt the sting of racial tension. As he describes it, "certain families didn't want their kids to play with you. We were known as 'those kids down the street.'"

As Gabriel got older, his interest in music became obvious. By the time he was thirteen years old, he was a member of the choir and had begun to play the saxophone, cello, and piano. How he came to play the guitar sprung from a moment Gabriel remembers clearly: His mother was voicing her pride to some family members about her son's gift for music, bragging about his talent. However, she incorrectly thought it was the guitar he played—"My son can play the guitar, right?"—and because he did not want her to look bad, he said "yeah." He had no idea that she was planning to buy him a guitar for his birthday.

A few weeks later, his birthday came around, and sure enough, Gabriel received the guitar from his mother. Knowing that he had told her he could play it, he sat looking at it, dumbfounded. When she asked him to play something for the family, he put her off. It didn't take long—a couple of days—for her to realize that he had lied to her. She told him to sell the guitar.

Instead, Gabriel put the guitar into his closet and nearly forgot about it for about a year. In fact, he would have forgotten about it completely had it not been for his mother's constant reminders. She repeatedly told him to sell it, telling him he could keep the money, instead of letting it just sit there and take up space. But Gabriel told her, "You know, one day I'm going to be a famous guitar player. I can't sell it! She was like, 'whatever.'"

Gabriel purchased some new guitar strings and found someone to help him string the instrument. At first strum he was hooked and knew the guitar would become an addiction, albeit a clean one. Later, he sometimes reminded his mom that she almost ended his career before it started. His mother laughs about the whole thing now, saying, "I wish you wouldn't tell people that story anymore."

Once Gabriel got started, he began "playing like crazy," but he admits he wasn't anywhere near being a prodigy. As he puts it, "I didn't just pick up the guitar and start playing Mozart." Getting good was going to take some work. He began to study the instrument in high school. He was able to read music because of his experience with other instruments. When he was fourteen, most of Gabriel's musical influence came from rock and roll and rhythm and blues. However, from the onset Gabriel did not feel challenged enough playing rock and roll; it just seemed a little too easy for him.

Feeling bored, Gabriel wondered what there was for him that would be more of a musical challenge. Fortunately for Gabriel and his future success, his teacher introduced him to classical guitar. Gabriel found that the notes were harder to read, and the technique of using all his right-hand fingertips on the strings instead of strumming up and down with a pick was more difficult. Ready to take on the challenge and try something different and outside the norm, he decided to give classical a try.

Although Gabriel knew he was getting a late start—most classical guitarists get started as early as six years old—at seventeen he really began to sink his teeth into the world of classical guitar. He practiced in high school every chance he had. Unfortunately, as his talent and skills developed, so did his ego. He thought he was "king of the castle" and "the best guitar player in the school." As he would discover, he was going to have to take a step back and practice some humility.

After he graduated from high school, Gabriel decided to apply to Del Mar, a two-year college in Corpus Christi, Texas. The school required an audition to determine the applicant's level of musicianship and for placement in a major. After his classical guitar audition, Gabriel received a response from the school that he hadn't expected. Del Mar told him that he was not advanced enough musically to pursue a music performance major. Instead, he would have to major in music education. Gabriel was furious, but it was just the jolt he needed.

He realized he hadn't prepared himself very well and was far behind other students in the music performance department. Although he had to, as he puts it, "eat tons of humble pie," the rejection made him want to work harder. He gave up his social life—hanging out with his buddies, going out to eighteen-and-over clubs, the entire scene—so he could push himself, so he would no longer be the "young kid at the bottom" and the worst musician in the department. He began practicing eight to ten hours a day.

Gabriel really poured on the steam; he practiced with the same ferocity of feeling that he had felt when he was rejected after his college audition. He recalls, "If I had ten minutes between classes, I would practice for ten minutes. During lunch, I would run to a practice room, look over my English work, and if I had five minutes left, I would practice for five minutes."

His hours of practice paid off. At the end of his semester, Gabriel played for his performance jury. When he finished his piece, they told him that he did indeed qualify for the music performance major. Rather than respond to them graciously, Gabriel copped an attitude and said something he would later regret: "You know, I told you that when I first started here." And he walked off the stage, angry that they hadn't believed in him from the beginning and knowing full well that they could take his scholarship away. Luckily for Gabriel, the jury laughed it off, saying, "It's good you're driven like that."

Gabriel apologized for his attitude and kept going full speed, practicing during every free moment. Two years later, he transferred to Texas A&M to obtain his bachelor of music degree. Here he was hired as an adjunct faculty member (Gabriel believes he may have been the youngest person to serve in this capacity). This meant that not only would he be teaching at both A&M and Del Mar, but that his teachers at A&M would also be his colleagues.

Gabriel's success didn't stop with his teaching positions; he served on committees for the university and won an Honors Concert Competition with his classical guitar performance. He continued to enter different competitions and did so well that he was offered scholarships to study for his master's degree at Cologne University in Germany and Austin Peay University in Clarksville, Tennessee.

Gabriel was flattered but felt drawn to an environment that offered more in the way of his Native American cultural identity. He applied to the University of Arizona in Tucson. As part of his application process, Gabriel traveled to Arizona to meet with an instructor who would conduct his audition. Dispensing with formalities, the instructor suggested having the audition at his house.

Gabriel remembers this audition as an event that would change the course of his career and life: "It was very low key. We walked to his house and I met his wife. He said, 'Let's have the audition.' I started playing and I saw him start fidgeting.

Gabriel Ayala

I thought, 'Man, he doesn't like me. He thinks I'm awful.'" While Gabriel was playing, the instructor reached for his cell phone and Gabriel thought, "Is this guy going to use the phone while I'm playing?" But the words Gabriel heard him say— "I accept Gabriel Ayala on a full graduate fellowship. I want everything to be covered for him."—just stopped Gabriel in his tracks. He recalls, "I thought, 'What just happened?' He was just smiling while I was freaking out."

As informal as the process was, Gabriel had just been accepted to the university. All he had to do at that point was start his paperwork and take his entrance exam. Receiving a full graduate scholarship meant he could attend school to study the guitar without having to serve as a teacher's assistant. When he traveled back to Texas to tell his instructors at A&M that he had just been offered a full graduate fellowship, they said, "Wow! You are getting a full ride."

So in 1995, after finishing his undergraduate studies, Gabriel prepared to make the long drive to Tucson, Arizona, filled with excitement and apprehension about what lay ahead. He packed his Bronco "to the roof" with guitars, clothes, and bookshelves and drove to Arizona, not knowing a soul there. He had no place to stay because his apartment wasn't ready, so he slept in the Bronco for a couple of days, showering at the school gym and practicing in the music room. At the end of the day he would return to his truck, "too proud" to ask fellow students or his professor for a place to stay.

Gabriel was tired and ready to begin his studies at his new school, but he still had to take his Graduate Record Examination (GRE), a standardized admissions test required by many graduate schools. But the day before the exam was to take place, a close relative of Gabriel's passed away, leaving him devastated and not up to taking the exam. He approached the university committee and expressed his desire to return home. He was told if he did not take the GRE, he would not be able to attend the university.

Gabriel felt sad and alone. He splurged on a hotel, then called his family, determined to return home. His uncle spoke on the phone to Gabriel and discouraged him: "You can't come home. I won't let you. We are proud of you and school is where you need to be. Keep going forward, don't go backward."

Gabriel decided to stay, but not without experiencing turmoil: "It was a rough night for me. I'd never been alone when a relative had passed away. I felt empty and alone. It was a whole new world for me." That night he played a little bit on his guitar and thought about his relative. The next morning he took his GRE and placed high enough to be admitted to the university.

Gabriel, on a full scholarship, knew he couldn't mess around—that was not a choice. He dug in his heels and finished graduate school in two years with a 4.0 grade-point average. In 1997, he received his master's of music degree, with an emphasis on performance, and was honored by being one of twenty-two musicians chosen to compete in an international guitar competition in Malibu, California.

Fresh out of graduate school, he tried to be a smart musician. He says, "I wasn't going to assume that I was just going to be a player of music and everyone was going to love me. I had to learn how to get my name out there." He began hitting the competition circuit, traveling all over the United States. He took every opportunity he had to network and introduce himself to people in the music industry. He played small gigs around his town, asking churches to use their spaces and then donating portions of the proceeds in return. "If I had one hundred people, I could pay my bills," remembers Gabriel.

After a few years, Gabriel felt ready to create a CD. In 2003, he released his first independently distributed album, self-titled *Gabriel Ayala*. The album was nominated for a Native American Music Awards (Nammy) Best Independent Recording that year. Gabriel was disappointed when he didn't win and realized he needed to raise his standards for his next album. This, he decided, would be a Christmas CD.

When he was growing up, the Christmas season was always big around his house. He says, "During Christmas, people would start coming to town and would stay for about a week or so. They would camp out in the backyard. I had an uncle living next door. My grandmother's birthday was New Year's Day and everyone would come to her house for New Year's Eve. I was able to see all my family all the time."

But now he lived in Tucson, and, being in demand to perform, he traveled a lot. Although every year he told his family he would be home for the Christmas season, he did not always make it. Appropriately, Gabriel took the title of one of the album's songs as the title of the CD: *I'll Be Home for Christmas*. And, even more appropriately, the final lyrics of the song express his sentiments exactly: "I'll be home for Christmas—if only in my dreams."

Gabriel worked extensively on the album. Finally feeling that it was ready and he was satisfied with the finished product, he released it to the world in 2007. He was proud of the CD, thinking, "This is the quality of material that I should be releasing," and with its release gained more confidence as an artist.

During the two years that Gabriel was creating *I'll Be Home for Christmas*, he was also exploring the tango style of music. He became passionate about playing and arranging it, and the idea occurred to him to create a tango-themed CD. In 2008, he did just that, independently releasing a CD simply titled *Tango!*, which received high marks from critics and garnered nominations in several categories from the Aboriginal Peoples Choice Music Awards in Canada.

Gabriel was on fire, doing almost everything he always wanted to do for his career. But one thing remained just beyond his reach: his desire to be signed with a recording company, namely Canyon Records.

Canyon has recorded and distributed traditional Native American music since 1951. The catch for Gabriel was that he did not play traditional Native music. When he originally contacted Canyon and asked to record with the label, he was turned down with the response,

Gabriel Ayala

"We do traditional Native music, and you are classical." Years later he contacted the people at Canyon again and told them, "I want to be a part of your company, and I'm not going away like other musicians." Finally, Gabriel received an email from them inviting him to Phoenix, where the recording company is located. Gabriel thought, "Beautiful!"

He spent a day recording with Canyon Records, demonstrating his musicianship in such classical styles as baroque and romantic. This was more than enough to convince Canyon. Shortly thereafter he received word that the recording company wanted to offer him a contract.

This was a change of direction for both parties involved. Up to this point in his life, Gabriel had been an independent artist with no outside influences impinging on his creativity. Canyon, on the other hand, had never worked with a Native American classical musician, or, for that matter, with any classical musician.

Canyon Records decided to create a separate division of musical offerings, known as the Explorer Series, to specialize in music beyond traditional Native American styles. The series focuses on two distinct categories: the classical music category, performed by Native artists, and world music, performed by indigenous cultures outside North America. Gabriel was asked to be the first musician in the classical music category. In 2008, he released his first album with Canyon Records, *Portraits*, which received fantastic critical reviews.

Gabriel's success as an artist is not only the result of working hard but also of making positive choices, including abstinence from drinking, smoking, and drugs. He has met and played with countless musicians on the road, including Mato Nanji of the popular band Indigenous, who commented, "We love your music, but what are you doing with your fingers?" While traveling extensively in the United States for his many performances, Gabriel still finds time to teach classical guitar to students as young as six and as old as seventy. He also promotes Native culture through traditional singing and dancing and has received awards in Arizona for being a positive role model for Native youth.

When he speaks to young people during his travels, he tells them to forgo drugs and alcohol as he has done. He lets them know that being born into the Native culture does not limit them—they can break stereotypes, as he did, and become doctors, lawyers, violinists, and composers, whatever they aspire to. After he speaks to them, he puts his guitar down, picks up a drum, and begins to sing traditional songs. The kids invariably say, "Wow, you can do both?" And Gabriel answers them with a resounding yes, telling them that this is what keeps him grounded.

In fact, he tries to live a traditional lifestyle all the time and credits his culture and his family with keeping him humble: "If I didn't have my culture, I would think I was a rock star, because it's easy to get wrapped up in this way of life. People want your autograph. They want to buy you things and give you things for free." At Native ceremonies, he is just another person and is not treated differently. He explains, "They don't say, 'Oh, there is that guitar-playing guy.' They say, 'There is Gabriel. Tell him to build a shelter; we need shade for our elders.' It is a good thing. It keeps me humble in my everyday life."

Gabriel sometimes finds it weird to share his stories: "As Native people, we are told that we are not supposed to talk about ourselves; it sounds like we're bragging." However, he believes that people need to realize that they are role models. This is serious to him, "a big deal," as he puts it, because if he messes up, he feels it gives young people permission to also mess up.

Gabriel Ayala—classical guitarist, music teacher, promoter of Native culture, and role model—continues to perform at numerous concerts throughout the United States and Canada.

Contact Gabriel Ayala
Website: www.ayalaguitarist.com
To write to Gabriel, sign up on the website.

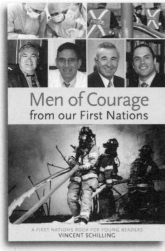

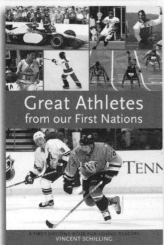
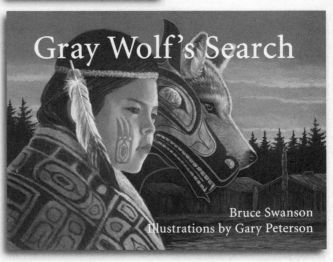